Contents

Atonal Improvisation and Jazz

A study of Chromatic Interval Pairs and Trichords

By

Jared E. Davis

Disclosure

This book is designed to help you explore a new way of thinking about music, improvisation, composition, and your instrument. We will be looking at a specific approach to Atonality and how to apply it to improvisation and the way you think about your instrument. We will be exploring the realm of chromatic intervals.

Throughout this book we will be referring to a system of applying the 12 chromatic notes to 12 numbers 0-11. Ex. C=0, C#=1, D=2 etc… However, we will be using a movable 0 system. Which means any note we start on is 0. So, starting on A, A=0 A#=1, and B=2 etc… (as opposed to C always being 0 and C# always being 1)

This is how we will count our intervals. All we are doing is counting how many half-steps our intervals are made of. For example, a Minor Third is a "3" and a Minor Second is a "1". Unison is a "0" and a Major Seventh is an "11". No matter what note we start on. Also, accidentals do not carry over on to other notes in a measure and we will not use any key signatures.

Minor second = 1	Perfect fifth = 7
Major second = 2	Minor sixth = 8
Minor third = 3	Major sixth = 9
Major third = 4	Minor seventh = 10
Perfect fourth = 5	Major seventh = 11
Tritone = 6	Unison/Octave = 0/12

Introduction

What does "Atonal" even mean? Most people usually describe the word "Atonal", as referring to 12-Tone music and constructing 12-Tone rows. However, the truth is that 12-Tone music is only one aspect of Atonality. Atonality simply means "that which is not Tonal". So really, it's just anything that cannot be described as "Tonal". For example, take the Whole-Tone scale. The Whole-Tone scale is not found naturally in a major or minor scale. If you were to write a piece of music using only the Whole-Tone scale, technically your piece would be Atonal.

Of course, that probably brings you to the question of "What about Modality? Are you Saying Modality is Atonal?" No, I'm not saying that. Modality is certainly different from classical Tonality, but they share many of the same defining characteristics. For example, they both use the same types of scales and chords. They both construct chords by stacking diatonic notes in thirds and they both have a Tonic center with chord functions. Even using modal mixture or modal interchange (borrowing chords from parallel modes) is a very common aspect of Tonality. Therefore, we cannot classify Modality as Atonal. So how do we make Atonal music that isn't 12-Tone?

If we take a look at music history, we can find that many composers were writing Atonal music before the idea of 12-Tone became common practice. How did they do it? Well, to say it simply, they just used intervals. They would construct new chords and scales from specific intervals. Going back to our Whole-Tone scale. This scale is made of Major Seconds only (2-2-2-2) and it happens to be symmetrical. Symmetrical scales like the Whole-Tone and the Octatonic/Symmetrical Diminished scale were another way that composers wrote Atonal music. The Octatonic scale or the Symmetrical Diminished scale, whichever you prefer to call it, is made of alternating Minor Seconds and Major Seconds (1-2-1-2) and is also symmetrical. Again, if you wrote a piece of music using only this scale, technically it would be Atonal. This was common among composers like Claude Debussy, Rimsky Korsakov and Modest Mussorgsky.

What about the other intervals? What if we include a Minor Third? What if we made a scale of only Minor Thirds and Minor Seconds (3-1-3-1)? Well, many composers already did back in the 1800s and it's called a Hexatonic scale. This scale is also symmetrical and has a very different sound than our other scales, because it isn't made of only whole-steps and half-steps. Now at the end of the day, all of these examples are still scales, and scales are a big aspect of Tonality. Also, limiting yourself to a fixed scale, especially a symmetrical one, doesn't leave you much room for experimentation and can feel harmonically static.

You may ask, why not use 12-Tone? Although it is fun and relatively easy to compose with, 12-Tone is very difficult to improvise with. You could memorize rows or possibly improvise a row very slowly, (if you can remember each of the notes you've already played as you go along) but for the most part it is completely impractical. So besides symmetrical scales and 12-Tone, what is left? The answer, Intervals only.

The method I will be discussing in this book is using specific intervals only to improvise and compose with. Intervallic writing was how composers like Arnold Schoenberg, Igor Stravinsky and Bela Bartok wrote Atonal music before and even after the idea of 12-Tone and Rows came about. For example, you might write a piece of music and are only allowed to use the intervals of Minor Second and Major Third. I call this two-interval technique "Interval Pairs".

I hope this exploration of Atonality gives you as much joy as it has given me!

Sincerely,

Jared

jareddavismusic.com   jareddavismusic.net

Instagram/YouTube: @jareddavismusic

Part I - Interval Pairs

Minor Second and Minor Third   (1-3)

Because most tonal scales are made of Minor and Major Seconds (1-2), we will skip over that pair and go straight to a mixture of Minor Seconds (1), and Minor Thirds (3). There are many different patterns you can create with these two intervals. You could play single interval stacks I call "Singulars" 1-1-1 giving us a fully chromatic scale, or 3-3-3 giving us fully diminished seventh arpeggios. You could play diminished seventh arpeggios connected by Minor Seconds or Minor Seconds connected by diminished arpeggios. You could alternate Minor Seconds and Minor Thirds, which would result in a symmetrical/hexatonic type scale. I suggest finding a few different licks to practice these intervals together, just so you can get them under your fingers.

Here are some little fragments or "Cells" you can practice to get the intervals under your fingers. Being a guitarist myself, we have many different ways to play the same intervals. Such as using only one string or two strings and choosing which fingers to use. Every instrument will have its own challenges, so feel free to experiment and find whatever works best for you.

-Practice shape 1

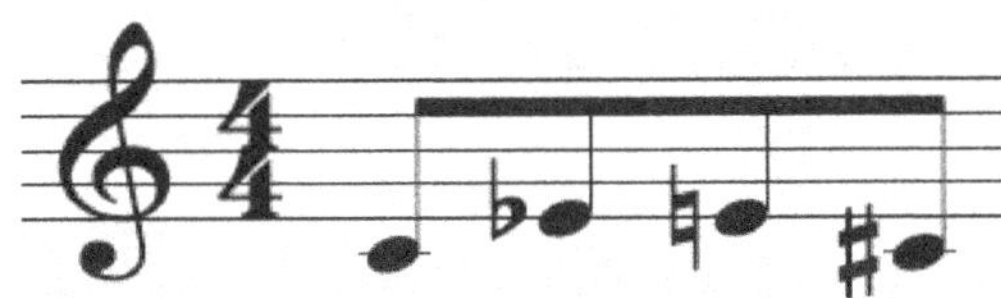

Try to move these patterns around your instrument, both forwards and backwards, to get used to the shapes in all positions, until you are comfortable with them. Remember it's not about playing these specific notes, or reading the music, it's about playing the intervals and visualizing them. You may start on any note.

You might also want to try some ascending and descending patterns that alternate between the two intervals. We will call this first technique "Alternation".

-Minor Second then Minor Third   1-3-1-3 Alternation

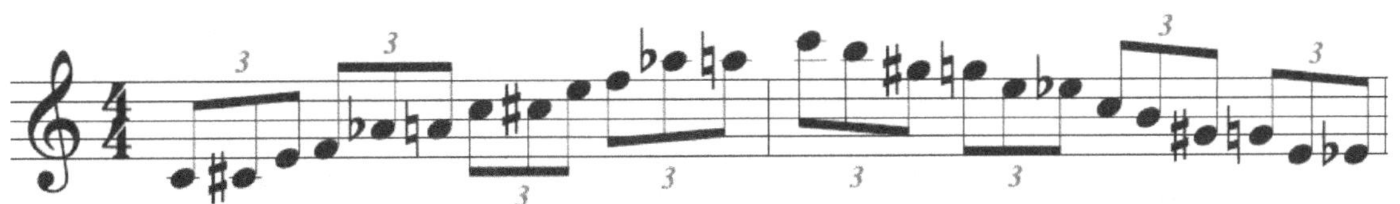

-Minor Third then Minor Second   3-1-3-1 Alternation

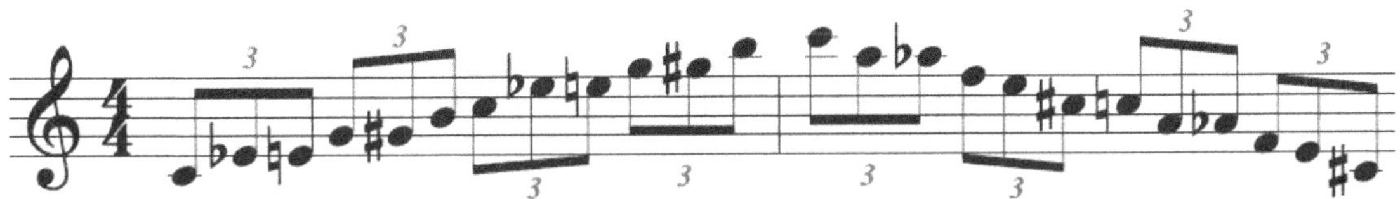

Another technique is "Pattern". Here is a 2121, or double-single pattern.

-2 Minor Thirds then 1 Minor Second.   3-3-1-3-3-1   2121 Pattern

Cell and Linking Interval

We can isolate some small fragments and use them to create longer lines. We will call these small fragments *cells* and then expand on each cell by adding a *linking interval* between them.

Ex.1. – Cell

Our cell is a Minor Second and Minor Third up, followed by a Minor Second down.

Ex. 2 – Ascending (linked by Minor Second down)

You can see the linking interval between each cell is a Minor Second down. From G to F#, A to G#, and B to A#.

Ex.3 – Ascending (liked by Minor Third up)

Here our linking interval is a Minor Third up. From G to Bb and from C# to E.

(Notice that we end up starting the cell over on the same pitch E an octave higher. This pattern is symmetrical and has created a Nicolas Slonimsky type line. One where we end up dividing the octave equally into two parts at the tritone.)

Problems To Watch Out For

This idea can be tricky to put into action and you need to be cautious not to include other intervals. Some patterns you might play simply out of intuition will seem right at first, but upon a closer examination you will find they include other intervals. Such as Minor Thirds descending or ascending by Minor Seconds.

-Minor Third shape descending by Minor Second.

Etc...

This pattern, although it may seem to work, actually does not because it contains a Major Third interval. From Eb to B, D to A# and C# to A are all Major Thirds. (Enharmonically spelled as Diminished Fourths)

The same problem would occur if the Minor Thirds were reversed, but now the uninvited interval is a Major Second. C to D, B to Db (Enharmonically), and Bb to C, are all Major Seconds.

Etc...

And this same problem would occur if we were to ascend as well.

Major Seconds between Eb and C# (Enharmonically), E to D, and F to Eb.

We can however fix this by alternating the direction we play our Minor Thirds.

Now we have eliminated all unwanted intervals and maintained our Minor Second ascension.

We can also reverse the interval direction and achieve a similar solution.

The same problems and solutions can be seen if we were to start with a Minor Second and move it by Minor Thirds.

This pattern actually creates the Symmetrical Diminished Scale, which again seems like it fits the criteria, however it too contains an uninvited interval of a Major Second. B to A, G# to F# and F to Eb are all Major Seconds.

Important Note

You may think I am being too strict about not including "wrong" intervals, but this is mostly just for the sake of theory and understanding. When it comes to improvising, we will not be robots and strictly follow the rules like this.

After learning these techniques and gaining some command over the intervals on your instrument, I strongly encourage you to practice free play with each pair. These techniques are designed to give you some direction. They are not the end goal. The end goal is for you to have new ideas and strategies to improvise and compose with the pairs.

Reconstructing II-V-I Lines

Okay I know what you are thinking, this seems fine and all, but how can we actually use these intervals to make coherent lines? A simple and very fun way to start is a technique I call "Reconstruction". We can take a line or lick that you already know and warp the notes to use only these intervals.

Any student of jazz knows that playing chromatically or playing outside is common, as long as you are sometimes hitting the correct chord tones in the correct places. You can simply start and end your lines on the correct chord tones. It really doesn't matter how far you stray away, once the listener hears the resolution to a chord tone, you will immediately be forgiven for all those "wrong" notes.

For example. Let's take a look at this basic II-V-I in C. We have a clear outlining of chord tones on the strong beats of 1 and 3. Notice how thematic it is. The theme is clearly arpeggios connected by steps. Very much like our Cells connected by a Linking Interval. Also notice the contour of the line. Two arpeggios up and then one arpeggio down.

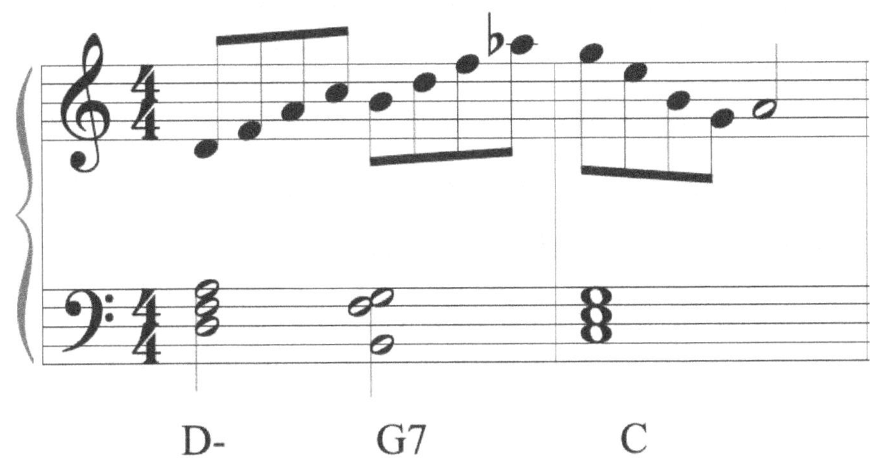

Now to make it fit our intervals of 1 and 3, all we have to do is try to maintain as many of these chord tones as we can and then alter all the other intervals to fit. Try to keep the same thematic material and contour of line as well.

So, you can see we still have the same thematic material and the same contour, but now the only intervals are Minor Seconds and Minor Thirds. Diminished arpeggios linked by half-steps. We did have to sacrifice some chord tones to make this work, but actually the A# works as a (#9) on G7 and the Gb works as a (b5) or (#11) on C.

Part of the reason using strict chromatic intervals is so great, is that you can make wrong notes sound right. For example, if we were to simply change the last note of the line to a "wrong note", it will still sound good because the consistent use of intervals creates such a strong continuity.

Starting the lick on D was a little tricky. We were able to keep the thematic material and the contour, but we had to sacrifice some chord tones. Starting the lick on F seems to work a bit better with maintaining the same chord tones and we can use some more interesting arpeggios than just a fully diminished seventh.

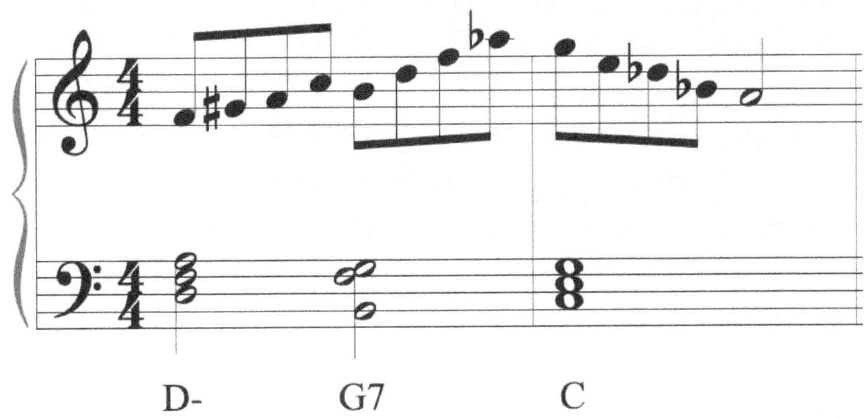

I suggest you try to write a few of your own II-V-I licks. An easy way to do this is to make a road map of the chord tones and then simply connect them with the chosen intervals. Remember, don't be afraid to land on some "wrong notes"!

List of Techniques and Interval Pairs

Let's recap the list of techniques I have introduced so far.

Singulars – Single interval stacks. Ex. 1-1-1-1 or 3-3-3-3

Alternation – Alternate between intervals. Ex. 1-3-1-3 or 3-1-3-1

Pattern – Different patterns between intervals. Ex. 2121/double single pattern

Cell – Small musical idea or fragment. See Ex.1 on Pg.10

Linking Interval – linking cells with a singular interval between them.

Reconstruction – Reconstructing a line or chord to contain desired intervals.

Here is a very strict full list of all 55 possible Interval Pairs.

1-2	1-3	1-4	1-5	1-6	1-7	1-8	1-9	1-10	1-11
	2-3	2-4	2-5	2-6	2-7	2-8	2-9	2-10	2-11
		3-4	3-5	3-6	3-7	3-8	3-9	3-10	3-11
			4-5	4-6	4-7	4-8	4-9	4-10	4-11
				5-6	5-7	5-8	5-9	5-10	5-11
					6-7	6-8	6-9	6-10	6-11
						7-8	7-9	7-10	7-11
							8-9	8-10	8-11
								9-10	9-11
									10-11

Octave Equivalency and Essential Pairs

Since 55 pairs is a very large number to work with, I have mapped out a way to reduce the number down to just a few I call the *Essential Pairs*. We can do so by using the *Octave Equivalency* rule. Octave Equivalency has been used in 12-tone music for over 100 years. It simply means that the interval number doesn't change if you jump up or down an octave. If C = 0 and you want a 4 to follow it, you can go up 4 to E or down 4 to Ab. Any E or Ab will be a 4 no matter how many octaves away it is from your original "0" C.

Semi-Tone full count

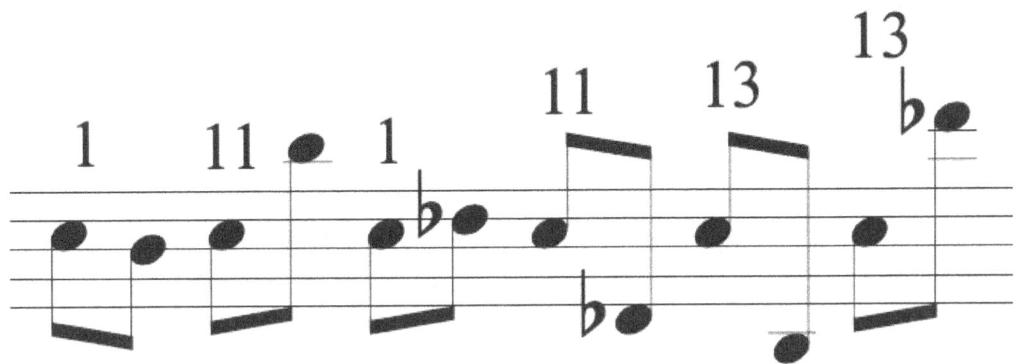

Octave Equivalent count

When we apply this to our intervals 1-11, it is reduced to 1-6. This is basically eliminating the inversions of intervals. For example, if C = 0 and we go down 1 to B, B = 1, but if we jump up an octave B = 11. Here is a list of the intervallic inversions.

Minor Second 1 = 11 Major Seventh

Major Second 2 = 10 Minor Seventh

Minor Third 3 = 9 Major Sixth

Major Third 4 = 8 Minor Sixth

Perfect Forth 5 = 7 Perfect Fifth

Tritone / Sharp Four 6 = 6 Flat Fifth / Tritone

Tip: Intervallic inversions always add up to 12.

Without the larger inversions, we are only left with 1-6. Giving us a smaller list of only 15 possible Interval Pairs, the "Essential Pairs".

1-2 1-3 1-4 1-5 1-6

2-3 2-4 2-5 2-6

3-4 3-5 3-6

4-5 4-6

5-6

We can also reduce the Essential Pairs even further by removing "Redundant Pairs". A redundant pair would be a pair where the first number is half of the second. For example, 1-2, 2-4, 3-6.

Of course, it is entirely up to you if you do want to use those pairs or not, but I personally find them to be too limiting. Additionally, I find pairs like 4-5, 4-6, 5-6 to also be limiting and difficult to work with. There are certainly some cool possibilities for material with them (especially chords) and they are worth exploring, but for improvisational purposes I rarely use them.

1-3 1-4 1-5 1-6

2-3 2-5 2-6

3-4 3-5

This list is the most realistic and practical in my opinion. So, let's explore each one of these Interval Pairs!

Example of Arnold Schoenberg using interval pair 3-4. Taken from *Pierre Lunaire, Der Kranke Monde,* M.22

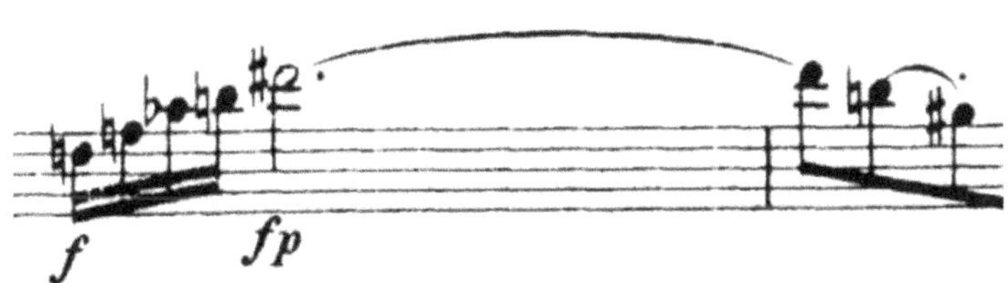

Minor Third + Major Third (3-4)

Since we already covered 1-3, we will start with 1-4 and explore each of the different techniques in the same order as before. This pair has Minor Seconds (1) and Major Thirds (4). Which means we can have Singulars of 1-1-1 giving us the fully chromatic scale or 4-4-4 giving us augmented arpeggios. So, you could think of having augmented arpeggios connected by half-steps or vice versa. Here are the same types of Cells or practice shapes like we did before.

-Practice Shape 1

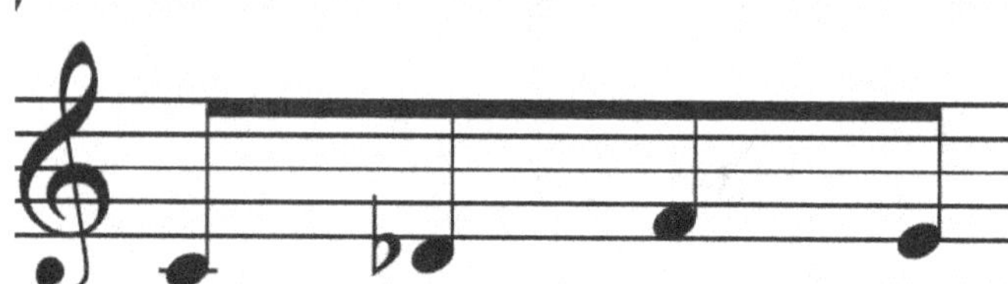

Etc…   1-4-1   Etc…

-Practice Shape 2

Etc…   4-1-4   Etc…

Remember to practice these forwards and backwards, and in all positions of your instrument. Also, remember the notes are not important, move these shapes to any starting note once you have them under your fingers.

-Minor Second then Major Third.   1-4-1-4 Alternation

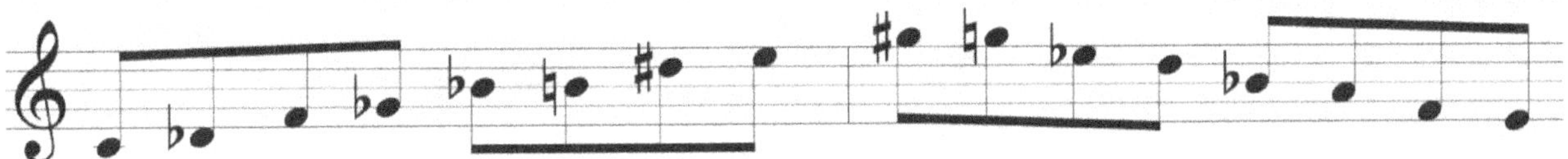

- Major Third then Minor Second.   4-1-4-1 Alternation

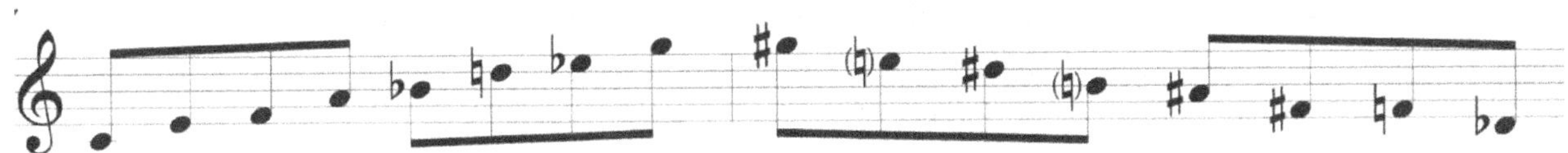

-2 Major Thirds then 1 Minor Second. 4-4-1-4-4-1   2121 Pattern

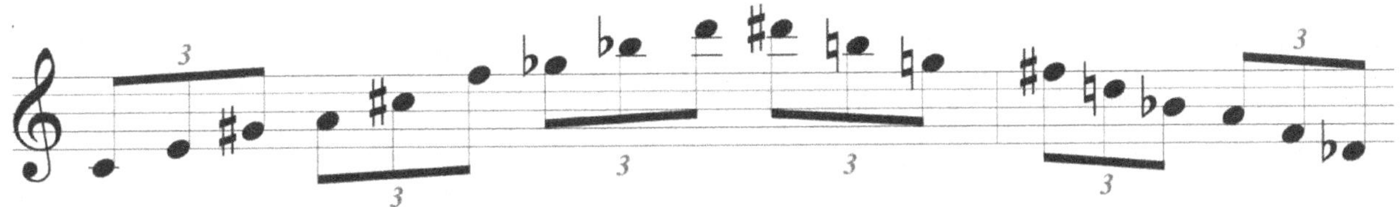

Cell and Linking Interval

Cell = minor second up + major third up + minor second down

Cell linked by major thirds up. This one is also Slonimsky like, it repeats two octaves up.

Cell linked by minor seconds down. Again, surprisingly by coincidence, this one repeats at the next octave.

Reconstruction

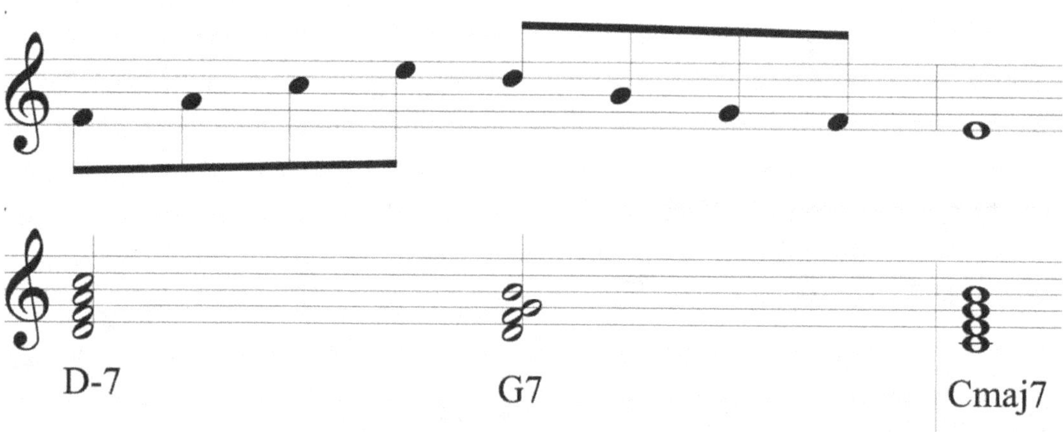

Here is a typical ii-V-I line, just like we did before. We will use this same line as a starting point for all the reconstructed ii-V-I lines going forward.

And here is the line reconstructed to only contain 1-4 intervals.

Example of A. Schoenberg using interval pair 1-5, taken from *George Lieder - Op.15, M.12*.

P4 + Minor Second   (1-5)

Minor Second and Perfect Fourth   (1-5)

This pair has Minor Seconds (1) and Perfect Fourths (5). As singulars we have 1-1-1 giving us the fully chromatic scale and 5-5-5 giving us quartal arpeggios. So, you can have quartal arpeggios connected by half-steps or vice versa. Here are the cells to use as practice shapes.

-Practice Shape 1

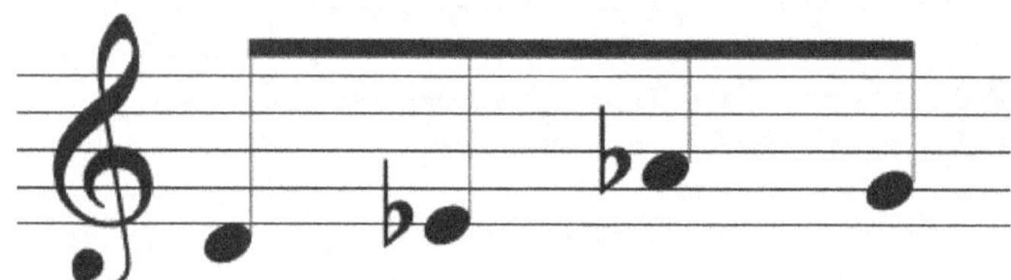

Etc… 1-5-1 Etc…

-Practice Shape 2

Etc… 5-1-5 Etc…

-Minor Second then Perfect Fourth.   1-5-1-5 Alternation

- Perfect Fourth then Minor Second.   5-1-5-1 Alternation

-2 Perfect Fourths then 1 Minor Second.   5-5-1-5-5-1   2121 Pattern

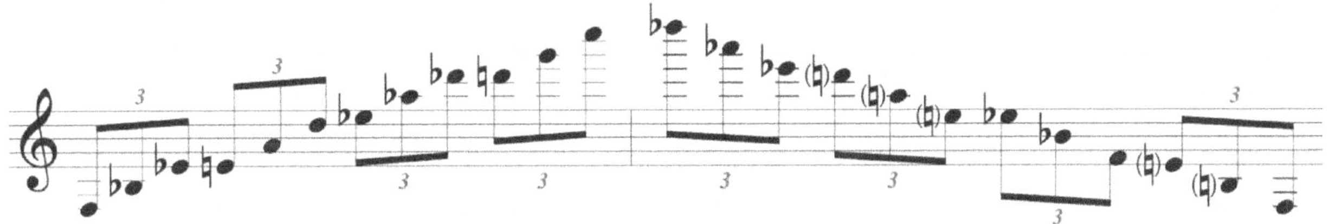

Cell and Linking Interval

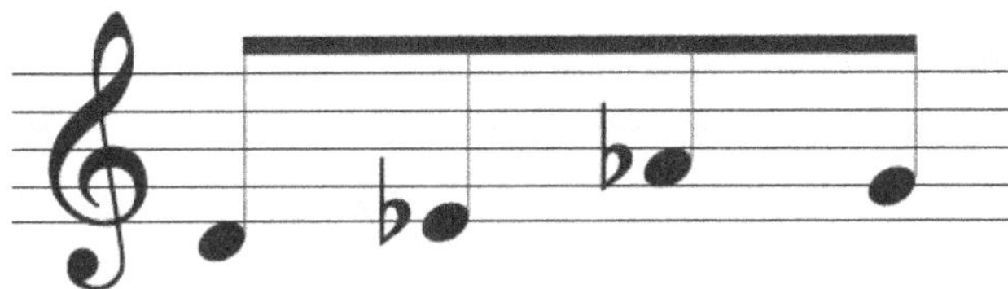

Cell = minor second up + perfect fourth up + minor second down

Cell linked by minor seconds down. This one repeats up an octave after three cycles.

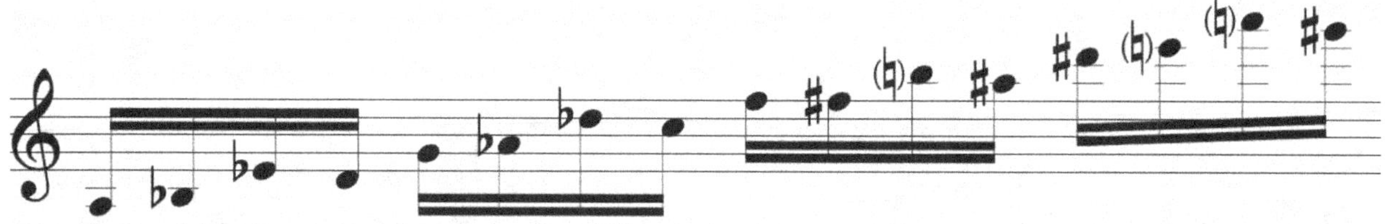

Cell linked by perfect fourths up.

Reconstruction

Here is our ii-V-I line reconstructed to only contain 1-5 intervals.

Minor Second and Tritone   (1-6)

This pair has Minor Seconds (1) and Tritones (6). As singulars we have 1-1-1 giving us the fully chromatic scale and 6-6-6 giving us tritone arpeggios. So, you can have tritone arpeggios connected by half-steps or vice versa. Here are the cells to use as practice shapes.

-Practice Shape 1

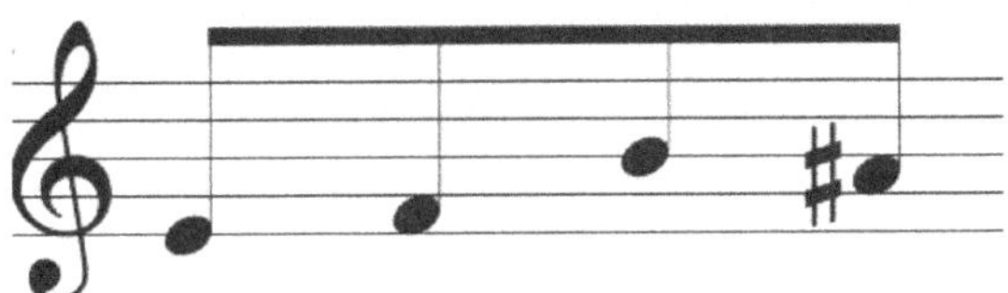

Etc…   1-6-1   Etc…

-Practice Shape 2

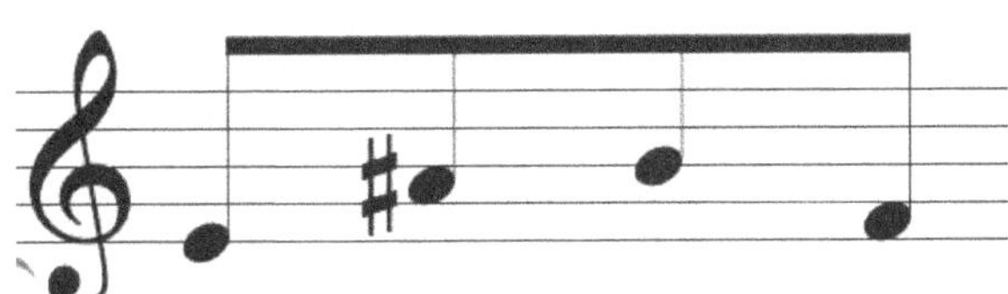

Etc… 6-1-6   Etc…

-Minor Second then Tritone.   1-6-1-6 Alternation

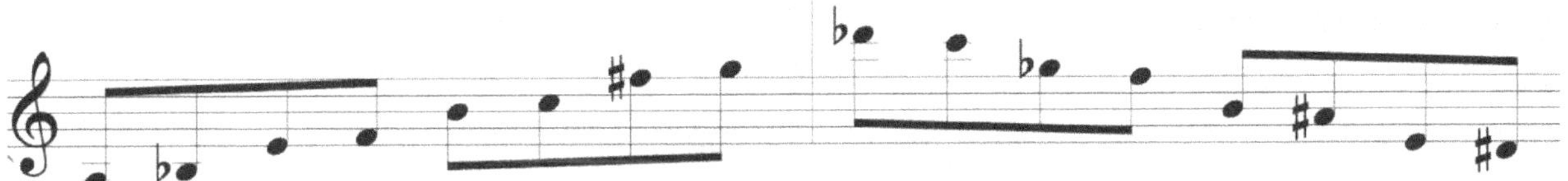

-Tritone then Minor Second.   6-1-6-1 Alternation

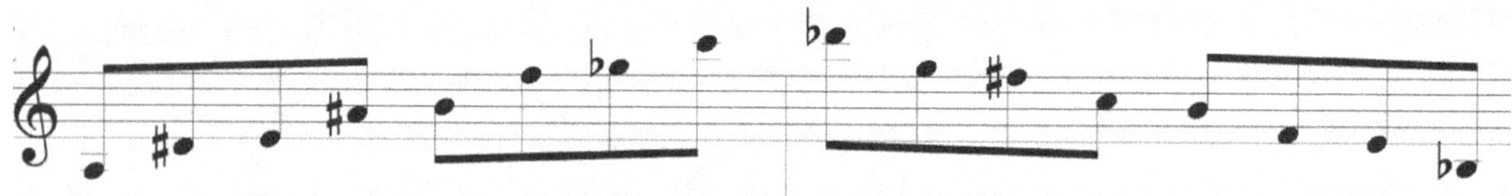

-2 Tritones then 1 Minor Second.   6-6-1-6-6-1   2121 Pattern

Cell and Linking Interval

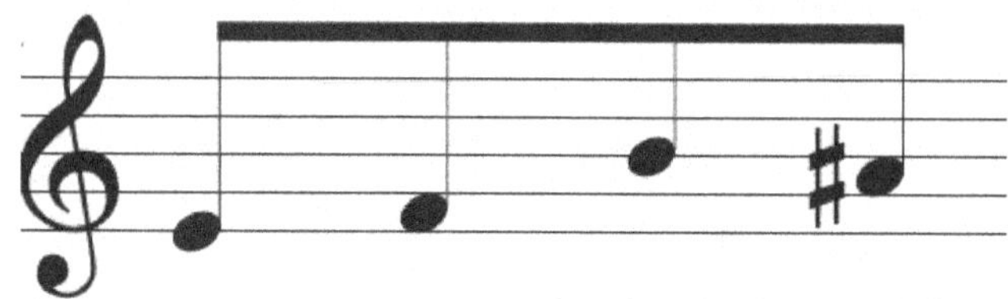

Cell = minor second up + tritone up + minor second down

Cell linked by minor seconds down. This one follows the cycle of 4ths.

Cell linked by tritones up. As you can see, this linking interval repeats the same cell each octave.

Reconstruction

Here is our ii-V-I line reconstructed to only contain 1-6 intervals. Notice we land on a #9/b3 over Cmaj7. Traditionally this would not be an appropriate chord tone to land on, but the intervallic consistency allows our ears hear this work.

Major Second and Minor Third   (2-3)

This pair has Major Seconds (2) and Minor Thirds (3). Which means we can have Singulars of 2-2-2 giving us the whole-tone scale or 3-3-3 giving us diminished arpeggios. So, you could think of having diminished arpeggios connected by whole-steps or vice versa. Here are the same types of Cells or practice shapes like we did before.

-Practice Shape 1

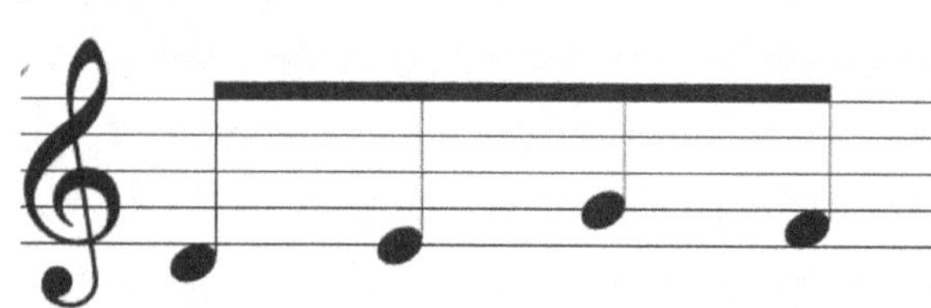

Etc... 2-3-2 Etc...

-Practice Shape 2

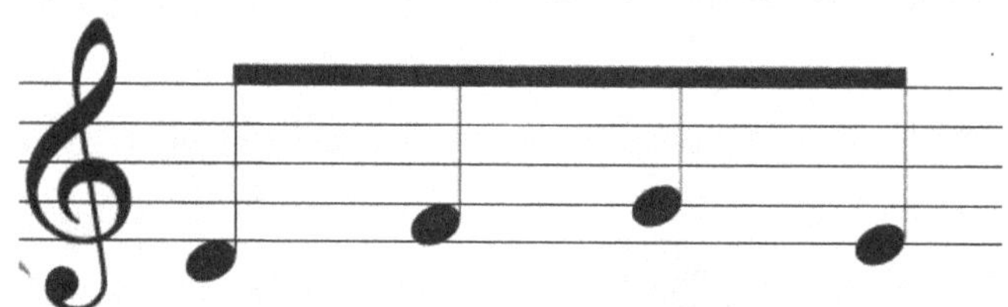

Etc... 3-2-3   Etc...

-Major Second then Minor Third.   2-3-2-3 Alternation

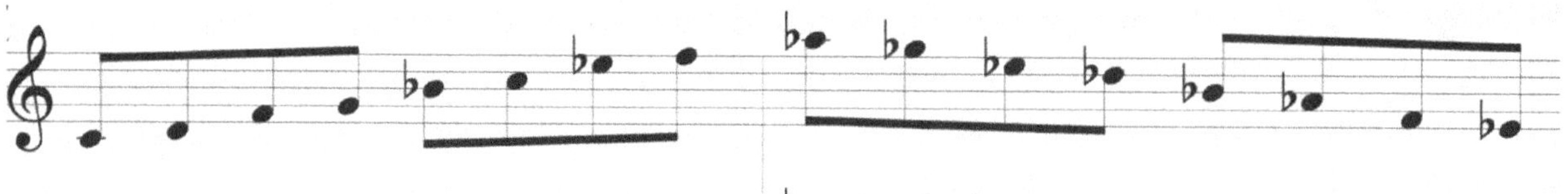

-Minor Third then Major Second.   3-2-3-2 Alternation

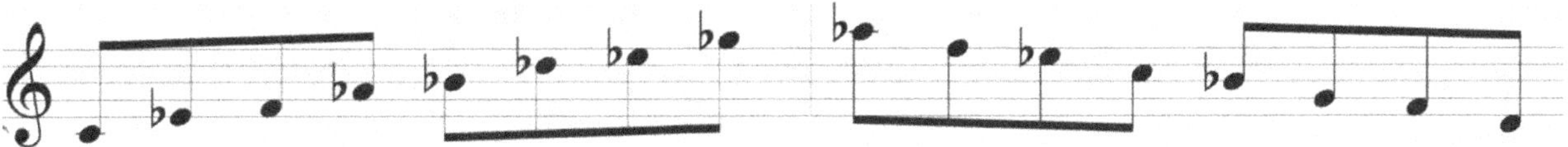

-2 Minor Thirds then 1 Major Second. 3-3-2-3-3-2   2121 Pattern

Cell and Linking Interval

Cell = minor third up + major second up + minor third down

Cell linked by major seconds up. This one is repeats at the next octave.

Cell linked by minor thirds up. This one follows the cycle of 4ths.

Reconstruction

Here is our ii-V-I line reconstructed to only contain 2-3 intervals. Although we landed on the 9th over the Cmaj7, we could have also landed on the #9/b3 using a 2 from F to Eb like we did in the last pair.

Major Second and Perfect Fourth   (2-5)

This pair has Major Seconds (2) and Perfect Fourths (5). Which means we can have Singulars of 2-2-2 giving us the whole-tone scale or 5-5-5 giving us quartal arpeggios. So, you could think of having quartal arpeggios connected by whole-steps or vice versa. Here are the same types of Cells or practice shapes like we did before.

-Practice Shape 1

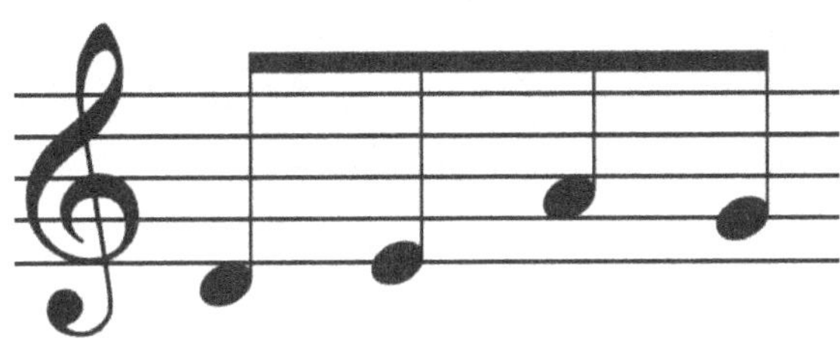

Etc...   2-5-2   Etc...

-Practice Shape 2

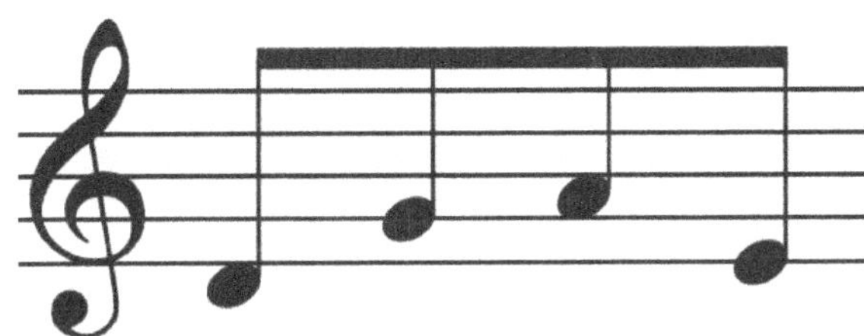

Etc...   5-2-5   Etc...

-Major Second then Perfect Fourth.   2-5-2-5 Alternation

- Perfect Fourth then Major Second.   5-2-5-2 Alternation

-2 Major Seconds then 1 Perfect Fourth.   2-2-5-2-2-5   2121 Pattern

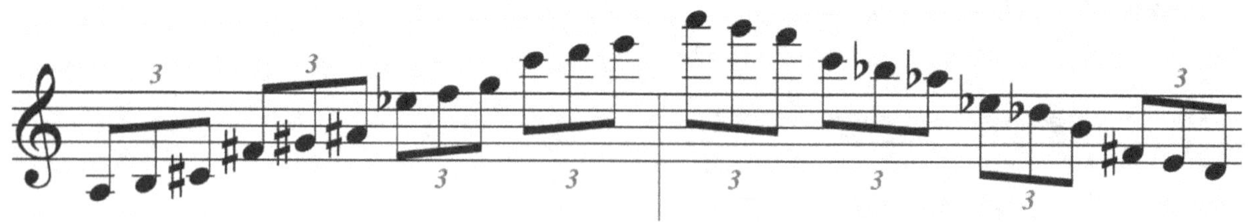

Cell and Linking Interval

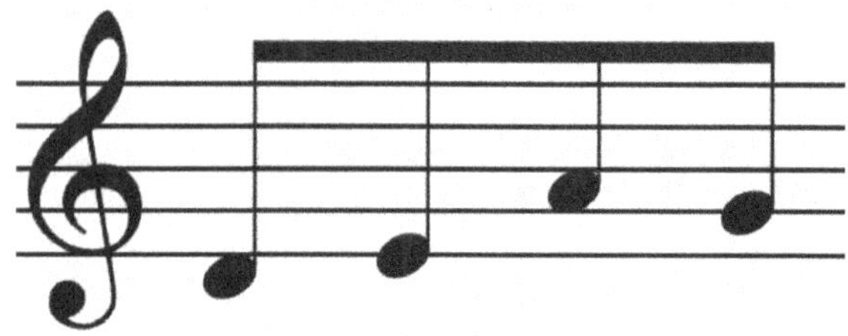

Cell = major second up + perfect fourth up + major second down

Cell linked by major seconds down. This one would repeat at the next octave after 4 cycles.

Cell linked by perfect fourths up. This one follows a descending whole-tone scale.

Reconstruction

Here is our ii-V-I line reconstructed to only contain 2-5 intervals. This line gave us a 9, b6 and b5 over G7.

Major Second and Tritone   (2-6)

This pair has Major Seconds (2) and Tritones (6). Which means we can have Singulars of 2-2-2 giving us the whole-tone scale or 6-6-6 giving us tritone arpeggios. So, you could think of having tritone arpeggios connected by whole-steps or vice versa. Here are the same types of Cells or practice shapes like we did before.

-Practice Shape 1

Etc...   2-6-2   Etc...

-Practice Shape 2

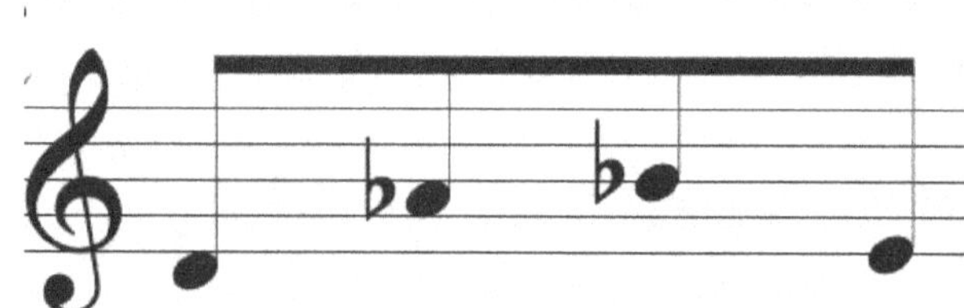

Etc...   6-2-6   Etc...

-Major Second then Tritone.   2-6-2-6 Alternation

-Tritone then Major Second.   6-2-6-2 Alternation

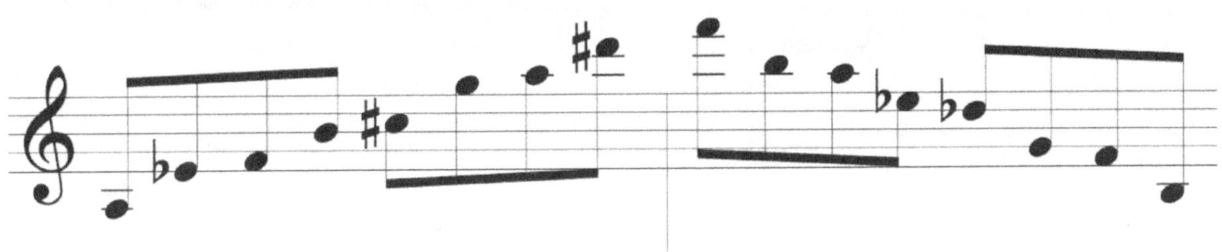

-2 Major Seconds then 1 Tritone.   2-2-6-2-2-6   2121 Pattern

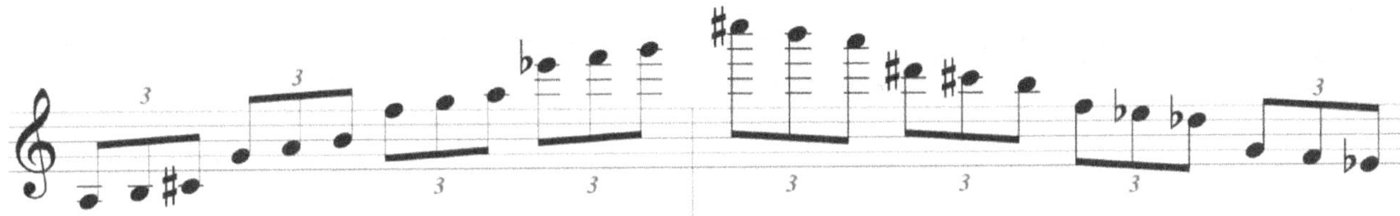

Cell and Linking Interval

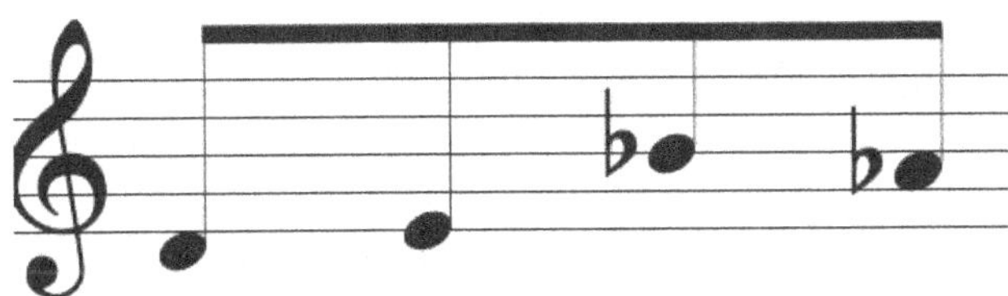

Cell = major second up + tritone up + major second down

Cell linked by major seconds down. This one repeats at the next octave after 3 cycles.

Cell linked by major seconds up. This one repeats two octaves up after 3 cycles as well.

Reconstruction

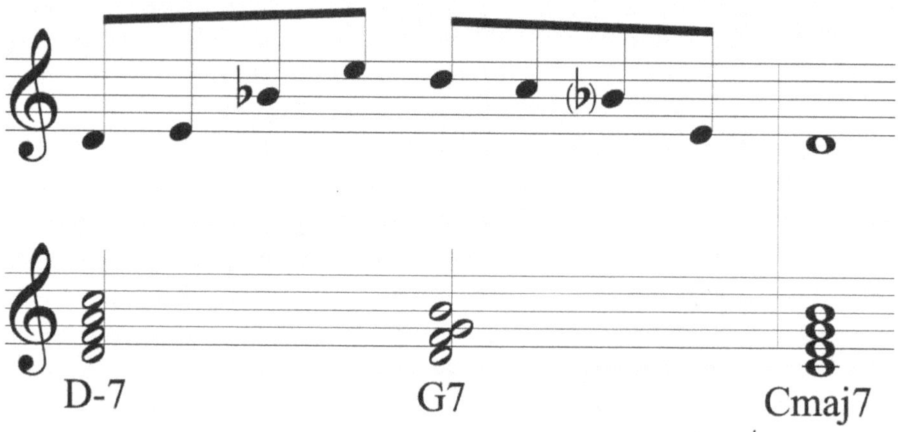

Here is our ii-V-I line reconstructed to only contain 2-6 intervals. This one gave us #9 and 13 over G7.

Minor Third and Major Third   (3-4)

This pair has Minor Thirds (3) and Major Thirds (4). Which means we can have Singulars of 3-3-3 giving us fully diminished arpeggios or 4-4-4 giving us augmented arpeggios. So, you could think of having augmented arpeggios connected by fully diminished arpeggios or vice versa. Here are the same types of Cells or practice shapes like we did before.

-Practice Shape 1

Etc…   3-4-3   Etc…

-Practice Shape 2

Etc…   4-3-4   Etc…

-Minor Third then Major Third.   3-4-3-4 Alternation

-Major Third then Minor Third.   4-3-4-3 Alternation

-2 Minor Thirds then 1 Major Third.   3-3-4-3-3-4   2121 Pattern

Cell and Linking Interval

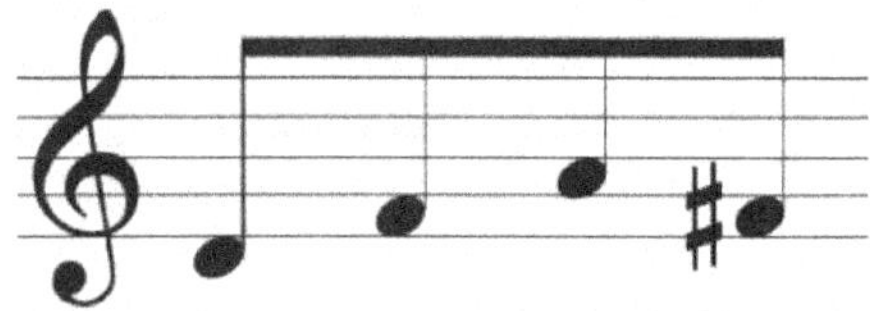

Cell = minor third up + major third up + minor third down

Cell linked by minor thirds up. This one follows the circle of 5ths.

Cell linked by minor thirds down. This one ascends by half-step.

Reconstruction

Here is our ii-V-I line reconstructed to only contain 3-4 intervals. This one gave us #4, and 9 over G7.

This pair has Minor Thirds (3) and Perfect Fourths (5). Which means we can have Singulars of 3-3-3 giving us fully diminished arpeggios or 5-5-5 giving us quartal arpeggios. So, you could think of having quartal arpeggios connected by fully diminished arpeggios or vice versa. Here are the same types of Cells or practice shapes like we did before.

-Practice Shape 1

Etc... 3-5-3 Etc...

-Practice Shape 2

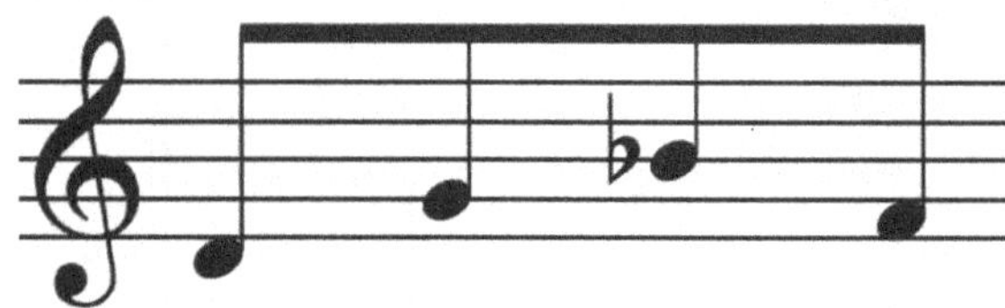

Etc... 5-3-5 Etc...

-Minor Third then Perfect Fourth.   3-5-3-5 Alternation

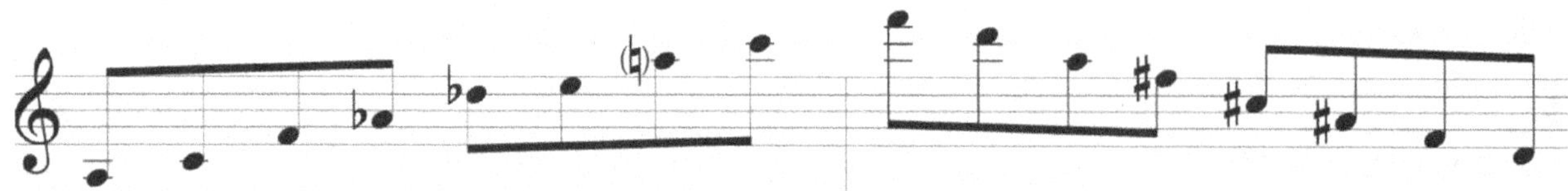

- Perfect Fourth then Minor Third.   5-3-5-3 Alternation

-2 Minor Thirds then 1 Perfect Fourth.   3-3-5-3-3-5   2121 Pattern

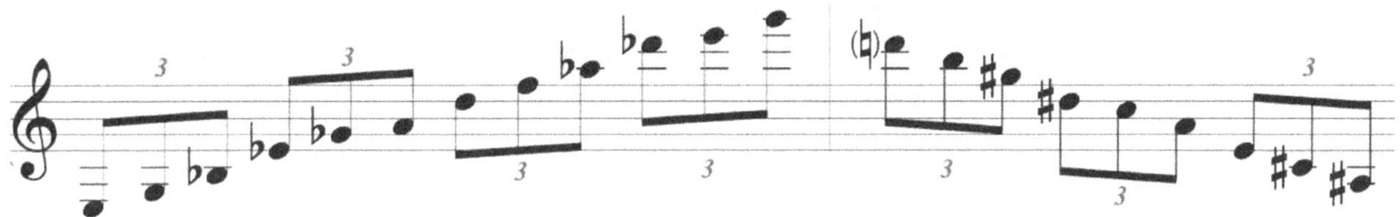

Cell and Linking Interval

Cell = minor third up + perfect fourth up + minor third down

Cell linked by minor thirds down. This one moves up by whole-steps.

Cell linked by minor thirds up. This one repeats after 3 cycles.

Reconstruction

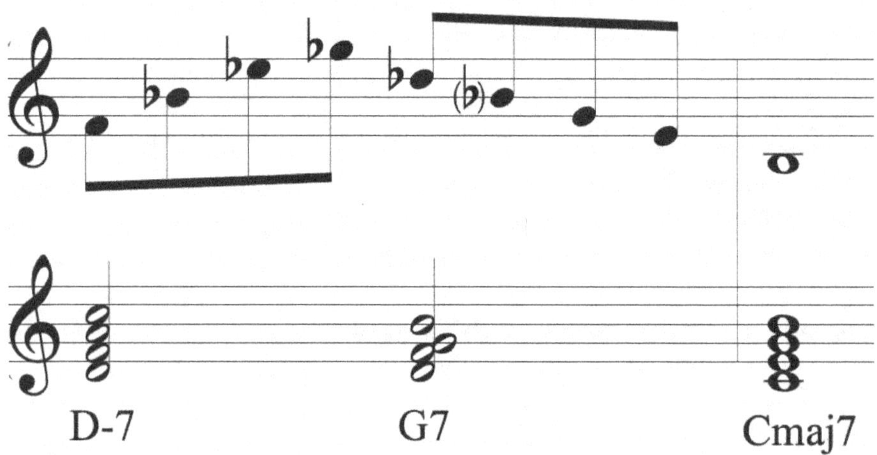

Here is our ii-V-I line reconstructed to only contain 3-5 intervals. This one gave us *b*5, #9, and 13 over G7.

Final Note

These examples have only demonstrated the smaller intervals in each pair, however adding octave displacement to any of these examples will yield the larger intervallic inversions of each pair. Which means each pair can also be thought of as having 4 intervals. Except pairs with 6, because 6 inverts to 6. Pairs with 6 will only have 3 intervals rather than 4.

$$1\text{-}3 \ = \ 11\text{-}9$$

$$1\text{-}4 \ = \ 11\text{-}8$$

$$1\text{-}5 \ = \ 11\text{-}7$$

$$2\text{-}3 \ = \ 10\text{-}9$$

$$2\text{-}5 \ = \ 10\text{-}7$$

$$3\text{-}4 \ = \ 9\text{-}8$$

$$3\text{-}5 \ = \ 9\text{-}7$$

$$1\text{-}6 \ = \ 11\text{-}6$$

$$2\text{-}6 \ = \ 10\text{-}6$$

Etudes

All of these techniques are designed to give you some language and open your mind to what is possible. However, the only way to master this new language is to compose and practice your own etudes. I have written out a short etude for each Interval Pair to guide you in the right direction, but playing through my etudes alone will not cut it. You MUST write your own etudes. It's the only way!

Etude 1-3

Etude   1-4

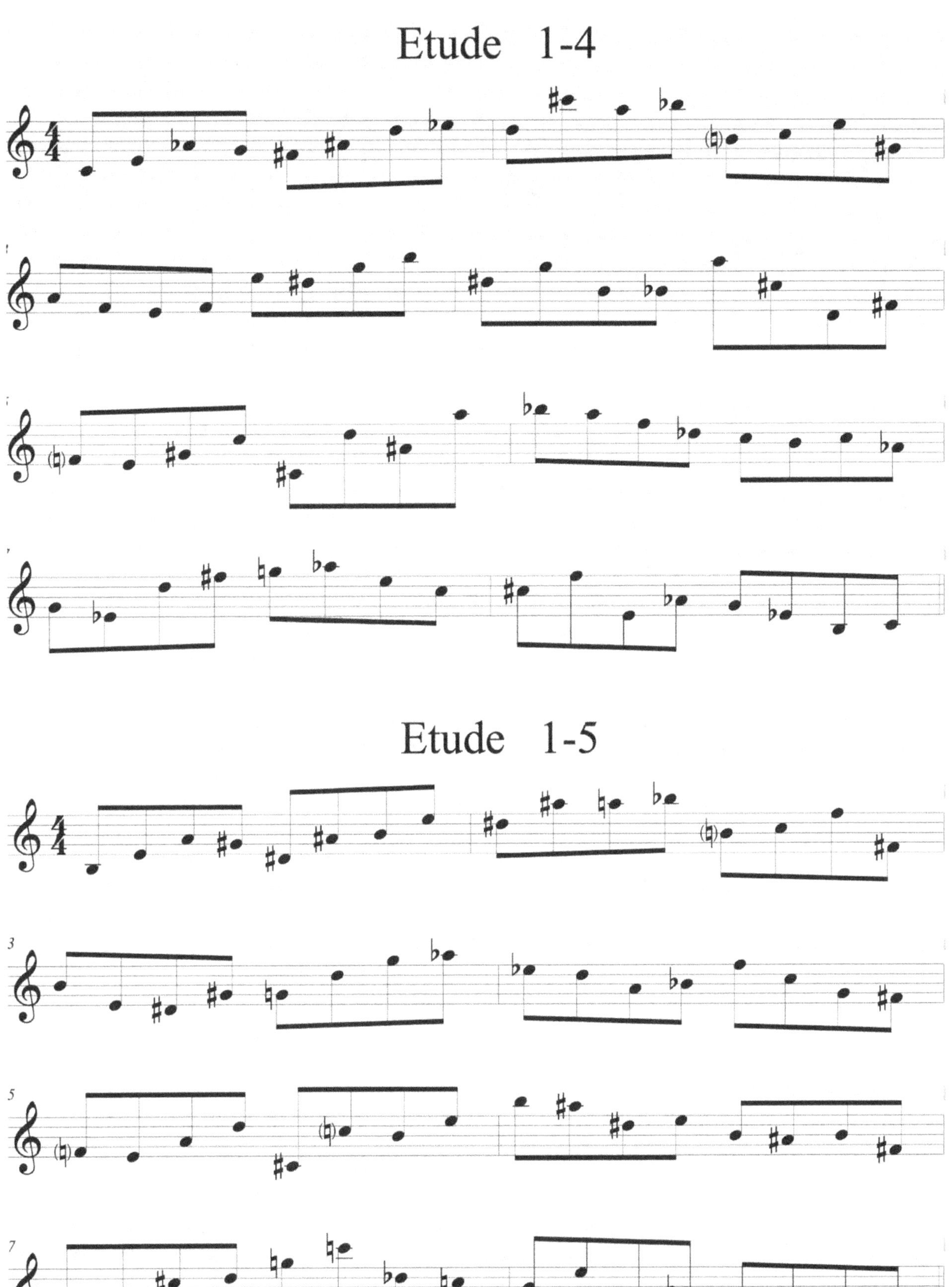

Etude   1-5

Etude 1-6

Etude 2-3

Etude 2-5

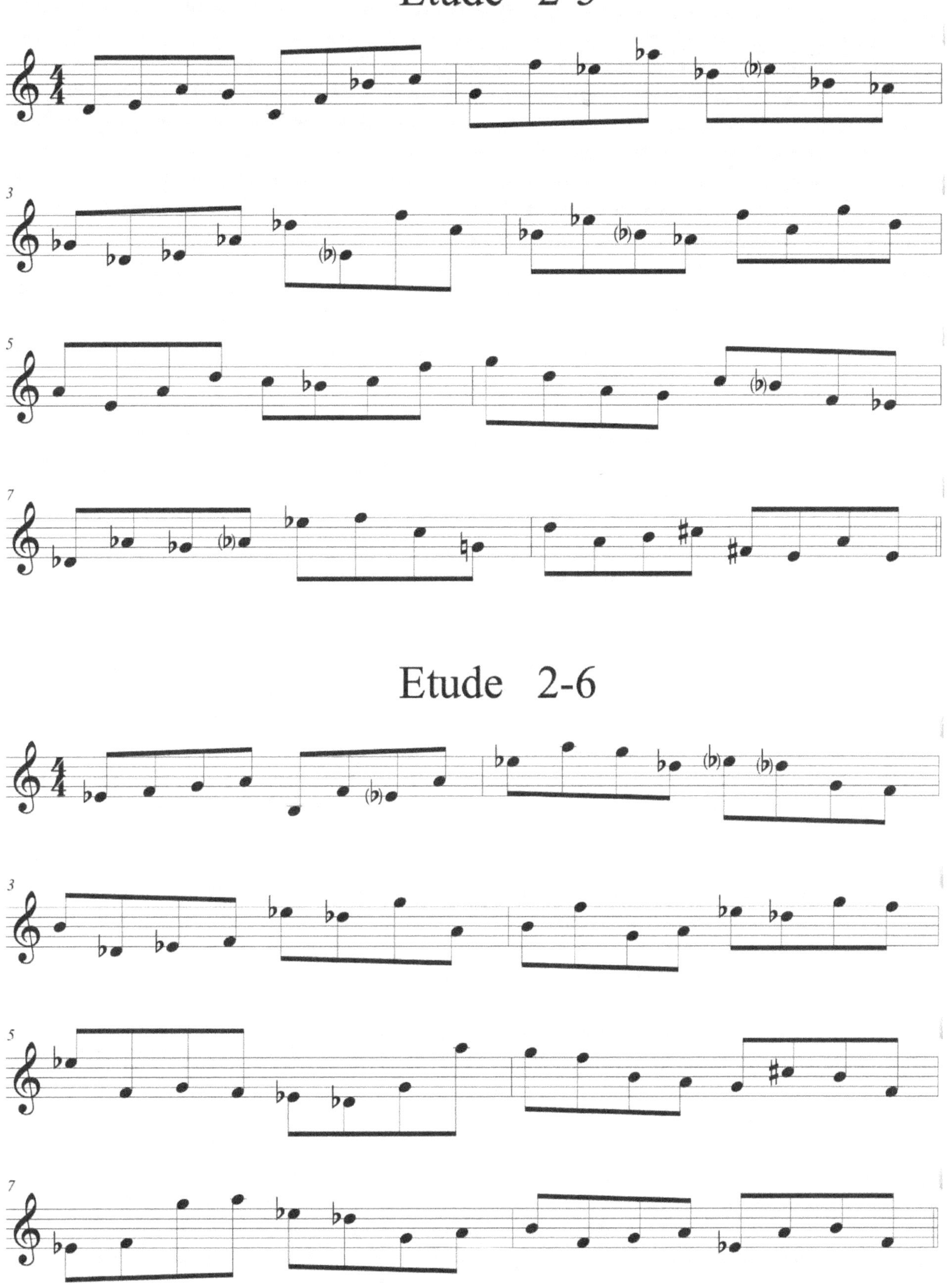

Etude 2-6

Etude   3-4

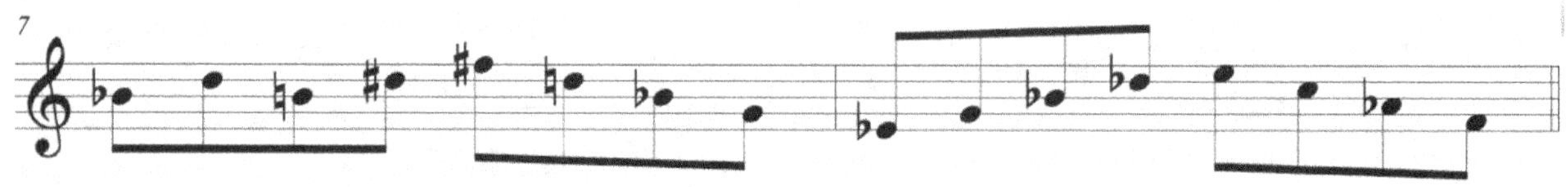

Etude   3-5

Part II – Trichords

In the Tonal world of music, triads are the smallest collection of notes you can have to make a chord.

1 note is just a note, 2 notes create an interval, and 3 notes make a triad.

The same principle holds true in the Atonal world.

1 note is still just a note, 2 notes still create an interval, but a collection of 3 notes in the Atonal world is called a "Trichord".

Trichords are one of the most essential tools for any Atonal composer. They are the smallest possible unit you can have when dealing with collections of pitches.

The symbols for trichords are very similar to the way we have been labelling our interval pairs. However, now we are adding in an additional interval.

"1-4" is the symbol for an interval pair of minor second + major third, but "014" is a trichord. Trichords are a single unit just like a triad. In the same way that a triad has 3 notes, trichords have 3 intervals.

The intervals contained in each trichord are called the "Interval Vector" and each trichord will always have an interval vector of 3 intervals.

In the same way that a C major triad (CEG) has 3 intervals, C-E is a major third, E-G is a minor third, and C-G is a perfect fifth.

In an 014 trichord, 0-1 is a minor second, 0-4 is a major third, but also 1-4 is a minor third.

So, the interval vector of 014 is 1-3-4, minor second + minor third + major third.

There is a total of 55 possible trichords if we use intervals 0-11.

Note

(In the atonal world it is common practice to use T for 10 and E for 11, however I found E to be problematic in certain situations as you will see later. Therefore, I opted to use L for 11 instead.)

55 Possible Trichords from 0 – 11 (L)

012 013 014 015 016 017 018 019 01T 01L

023 024 025 026 027 028 029 02T 02L

034 035 036 037 038 039 03T 03L

045 046 047 048 049 04T 04L

056 057 058 059 05T 05L

067 068 069 06T 06L

078 079 07T 07L

089 08T 08L

09T 09L

0TL

Of course, leaving out intervals larger than a tritone (6 half-steps), we have this fairly short list of 15 possible trichords. The *Essential Trichords*.

012 013 014 015 016

023 024 025 026

034 035 036

045 046

056

Allen Forte, who is one of the most important pioneers of atonal music, created a list of all possible pitch collections. In his list, which is commonly referred to as the "Forte List", he only lists these 12 possible trichords.

012 013 014 015 016

024 025 026 027

036 037

048

I find it a little perplexing that he went beyond the distance of a tritone, but his intentions for these pitch collections were very different than ours.

He was more focused on the actual notes in each trichord called the "Pitch Class Set", whereas for us, we are more focused on the intervals contained in them. Therefore, we can classify them as the "Interval Class Set".

Now, besides intervals extending past the tritone distance of 6, did you notice the additional difference between Forte's list and my list?

His list is missing trichords - 023 034 035 045 046 056

This is because these 6 trichords are redundant. Remember how we removed redundant pairs from our interval pair list?

Well, he essentially did the same thing with these 6. That's because these trichords are actually just the reverse orders of other trichords.

For example, take 023, if we imagine 3 is our 0, then moving from right to left, 023 is the same as 013.

0-1 = 1 and 3-2 = 1

1-3 = 2 and 2-0 = 2

0-3 = 3 and 3-0 = 3

013 and 023 both have the same interval vector of 1-2-3

The same is true of the other 5 trichords.

034 is the reverse of 014 and they share the same interval vector of 1-3-4

035 is the reverse of 025 and they share the same interval vector of 2-3-5

045 is the reverse of 015 and they share the same interval vector of 1-4-5

046 is the reverse of 026 and they share the same interval vector of 2-4-6

056 is the reverse of 016 and they share the same interval vector of 1-5-6

On top of removing these redundant pairs, for our purposes, we must also remove 012, 024 and 036. These trichords are also redundant because the second number is half of the third. Which means the interval vector of these trichords is actually only 2 intervals and not 3.

012 has an interval vector or 1-2

024 has an interval vector of 2-4

036 has an interval vector of 3-6

In the end, after removing all redundant trichords, we are only left with these 6.

013 014 015 016

025 026

Most of the previous techniques we covered can still be used with trichords, but of course now we have more options thanks to the third interval. It may seem like having 3 intervals to think about would be harder than 2, but I have found trichords to actually be much easier to improvise and compose with.

That is because interval pairs require more restrictions and a stronger attention to detail in order to avoid all the other "uninvited intervals". In fact, there are more than 3 times as many options because each trichord contains 3 interval pairs within them.

Without further a due, lets dive into these 6 trichords!

013

Our first trichord has three intervals contained in it.

1 = Minor Second

2 = Major Second

3 = Minor third

Which means its interval vector is 1-2-3.

So, we can have singulars of 1-1-1 giving us the fully chromatic scale, or 2-2-2 giving us the whole-tone scale, or 3-3-3 giving us fully diminished arpeggios, or any kind of alternation of the three like 1-2-1-2 or 1-3-1-3 or 2-3-2-3.

Which also means that there are 3 interval pairs of 1-2 1-3 2-3.

Literal

-Practice Shape 1

013 up, then 013 down.

This practice shape is taking the traditional pitch centric use of 013.
E = 0 F = 1 G = 3, then Ab = 0 G = 1 F = 3. This shape does not have a minor third
(3) between consecutive notes. I call this technique "Literal", because we take the
trichord literally.

Vector

-Practice Shape 2

1-2-3 up, then 1-2-3 down.

This practice shape is more focused on the interval vector. We play the vector 1-2-
3 up starting on E, then play it down starting from B. Minor Second (1) – Major
Second (2) – Minor Third (3). I call this technique "Vector", because we focus on
the vector intervals between consecutive notes instead of literal trichord pitches.

Chords

There are a few different ways we can think about creating chords. We can of
course use the stacking of the literal trichord or the vector. "Octave Equivalency"
allows for us to use inversions.

013 "Literal"

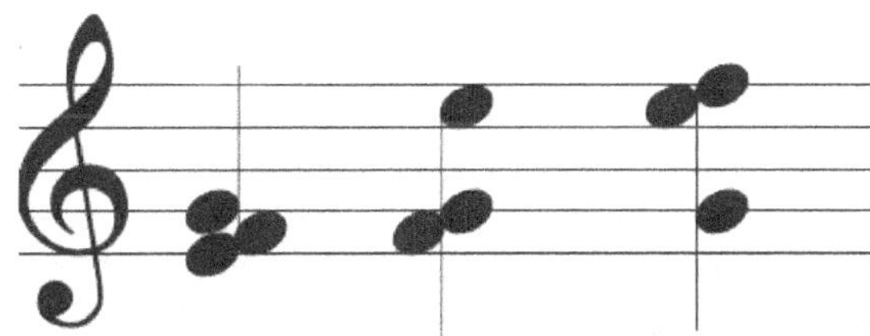

You can also use the reverse order or "Retrograde" of each trichord, for example 013 in reverse is 023. Just like we saw when we identified redundant trichords. We don't use 023 on its own because it's the retrograde of 013.

013 "Vector"

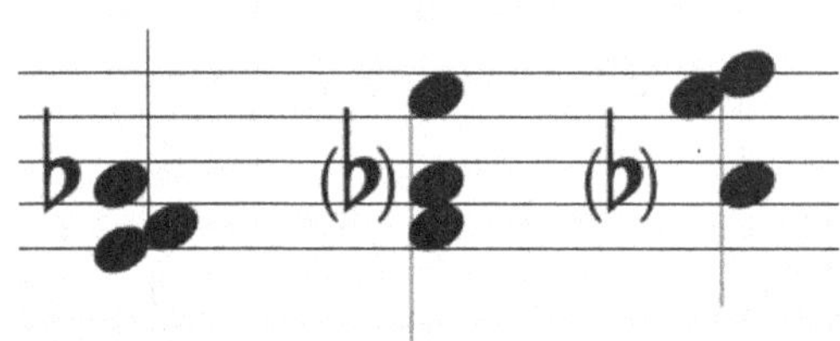

Vector trichords focus on intervals from vector.

You can make vector trichords out of any 2 intervals from the vector. You may also repeat a single interval twice like 1-1 or 2-2. You can also use the retrograde of any vector trichord, as long as it is not symmetrical. Symmetrical trichords will invert to the same intervals.

However, there are also some great ways to have symmetrical chords. We can easily turn a literal trichord into a symmetrical "Tetrachord" by adding the second number again after the third. For example, here we added 1 after 3 to make 0134.

0134 "Symm Tetrachord"

0134 is the same forward and backward.

1-2-3 "Vector Tetrachord"

A Vector Tetrachord can use all 3 intervals contained in each trichord. In this case 1-2-3. When using the vector, we measure consecutively from note to note, not from 0 to each note.

31013 Symm Pentachord

"Symmetrical Pentachords" are a little different than the symmetrical tetrachords, because the tetrachord is symmetrical from one end to the other, however the pentachord is not only symmetrical from one end to the other, but also from the center note moving out in both directions.

In this example A is the center pitch 0, moving 1-3 in both directions.

You can of course use the retrograde trichord versions of 023 for each tetra and pentachord.

Pairs of Pairs

Pairs of Pairs are exactly what they sound like. Instead of "interval" pairs, we use pairs of interval pairs. That means we can recycle some previous techniques like

Alternation or Pattern. Again, each trichord has 3 interval pairs within itself, and for 013, we have 1-2 1-3 2-3.

Which means we can have pairs of 1-2/1-3 1-2/2-3 1-3/2-3

Of course, I don't usually use the pair 1-2, but for the sake of understanding we will use it with 013.

1-3 / 1-2 Pair of Pair - Alternation

In this example we just used alternation between 1-3 and 1-2.

2-3 / 1-3 Pair of Pair - Pattern (2-2-3-1-3-3)

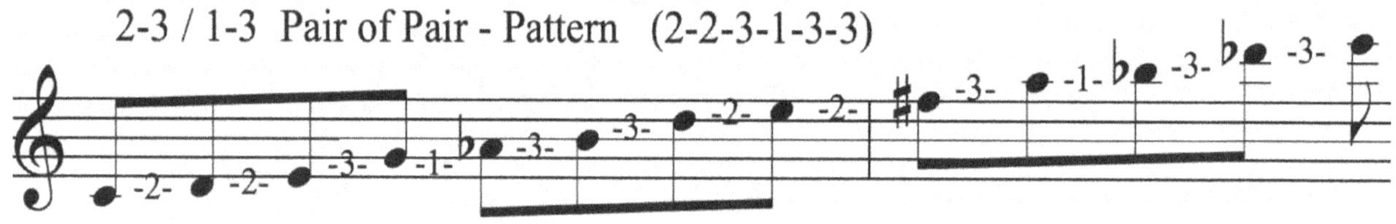

Patterns are another great tool for pairs of pairs. They can be as simple or as complex as desired. In this example the pattern is 2-2-3-1-3-3, which is essentially a more complex version of the 2121 pattern we saw with interval pairs.

Cell and Linking Interval

This technique is pretty much unchanged from how we used it with interval pairs, however now we have 3 intervals instead of 2 to work with. So, our cells can be a bit more complex. You can also create a cell from other techniques like literal, vector, retrograde or symmetrical chords.

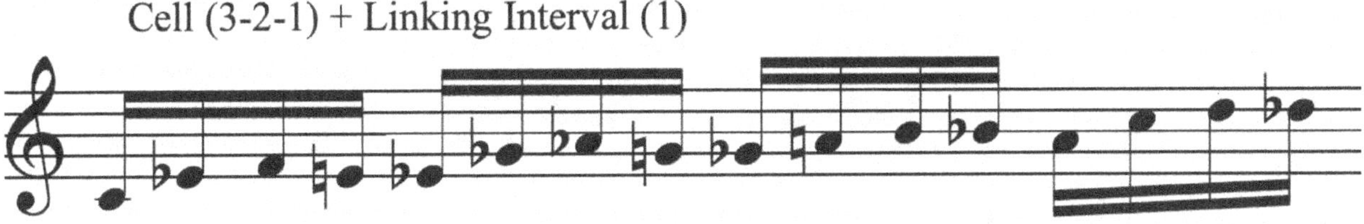

In this example our cell is 3-2-1 (3 up, 2 up, 1 down), linked by 1 down. This cell could essentially be described as a retrograde vector.

Reconstruction

This technique is also unchanged from how we learned it in part 1. Of course, the only difference is an additional interval, which yields far less restrictions than interval pairs.

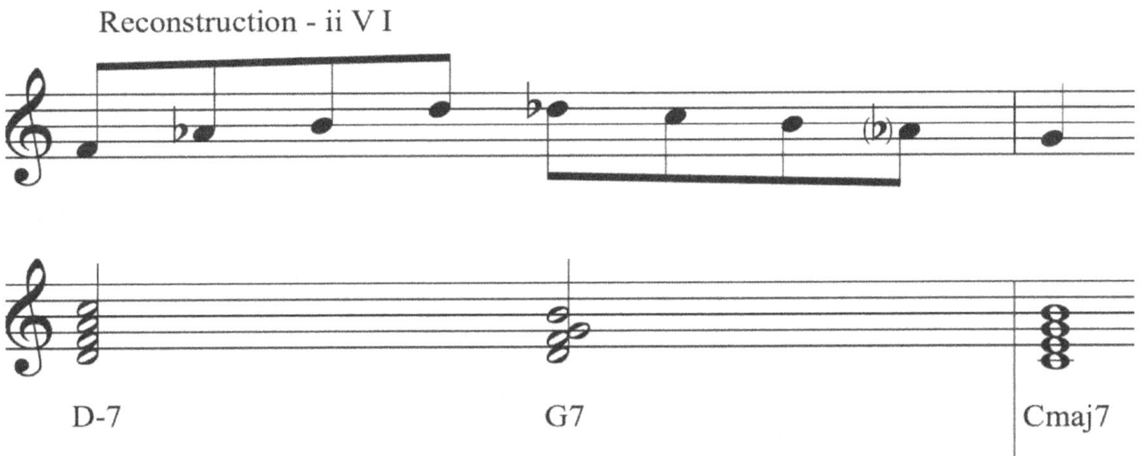

This reconstructed ii V I line only uses intervals from the 013 vector of 1-2-3.

List of Techniques

Let's recap the list of techniques we covered so far.

Literal Trichord - Trichord in the tradition pitch centric form.

Vector Trichord – Trichord created from intervals of its vector.

Retrograde Trichords – The reverse form of any trichord.

Symmetrical Tetrachord – 4-note chords that are the same in both directions.

Vector Tetrachord – 4-note chord created from intervals of the vector.

Symmetrical Pentachord – 5-note chord, symmetrical from center pitch out.

Pairs of Pairs *(Alternation + Pattern)* – Pairs of interval pairs.

Cell and Linking Interval – Small idea linked by a specific interval.

Reconstruction – Reconstructing "normal" lines or chords into trichords.

014

Our second trichord has these three intervals contained in it.

1 = Minor Second

3 = Minor third

4 = Major Third

Which means its interval vector is 1-3-4.

So, we can have singulars of 1-1-1 giving us the fully chromatic scale, or 3-3-3 giving us fully diminished arpeggios, or 4-4-4 giving us augmented arpeggios, or any kind of alternation of the three like 1-3-1-3 or 1-4-1-4 or 3-4-3-4.

Which also means that there are 3 interval pairs of 1-3 1-4 3-4.

Literal

-Practice Shape 1

014 up, then 014 down.

Vector

-Practice Shape 2

1-3-4 up, then 1-3-4 down.

Chords

Example of 014 from A. Schoenberg – George Lieder Op.15, M15-16

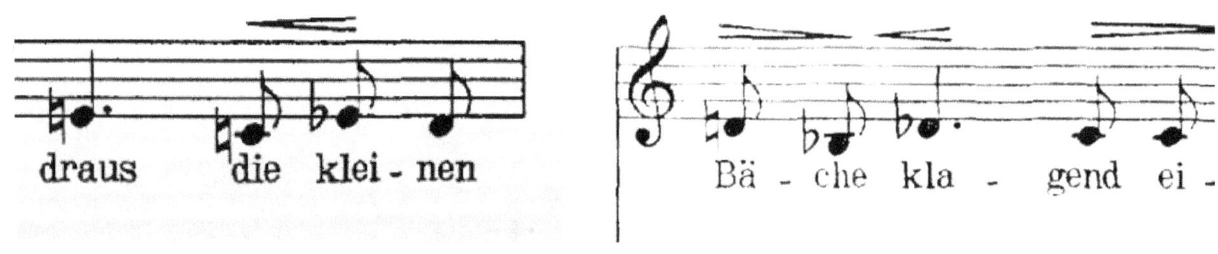

Intervals move 4-3-1, therefore the vector is 1-3-4 belonging to 014.

014 Vector

These vector trichords have more than one possibility. In this case, I chose to stack intervals 4-1 over the bass note, but you can do any combination of intervals from the vector.

0145 Symm Tetrachord

As we saw before, we can make the 014 symmetrical by adding a 1 to the end of it.

1-3-4 Vector Tetrachord

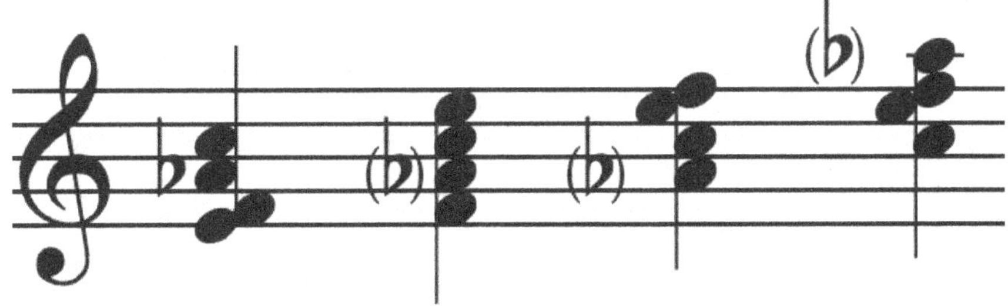

Here we stacked the vector 1-3-4 consecutively from note to note to create this tetrachord.

A is the center pitch 0, moving 1-4 in both directions creating this symmetrical pentachord.

You can also use the retrograde 034 for any of these tetrachords or pentachords.

Pairs of Pairs

As I mentioned before, the trichord 014 contains 3 interval pairs of   1-3   1-4   3-4.

Cell and Linking Interval

In this example we went 3-4-1 up as our cell, and down 4 for the linking interval.

Reconstruction

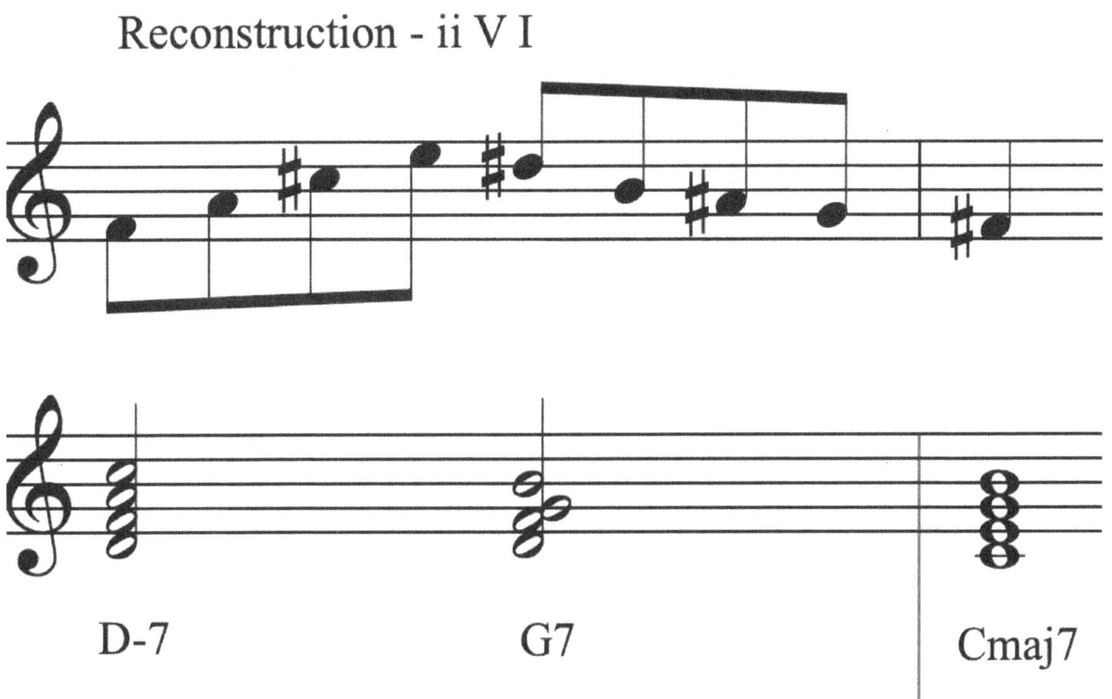

This reconstructed ii V I line only uses intervals from the 014 vector of 1-3-4.

015

Our third trichord has these three intervals contained in it.

1 = Minor Second

4 = Major Third

5 = Perfect Fourth

Which means its interval vector is 1-4-5.

So, we can have singulars of 1-1-1 giving us the fully chromatic scale, or 4-4-4 giving us augmented arpeggios, or 5-5-5 giving us quartal arpeggios, or any kind of alternation of the three like 1-4-1-4 or 1-5-1-5 or 4-5-4-5.

Which also means that there are 3 interval pairs of 1-4 1-5 4-5.

Literal

-Practice Shape 1

015 up, then 015 down.

Vector

-Practice Shape 2

1-4-5 up, then 1-4-5 down.

Chords

015 Literal

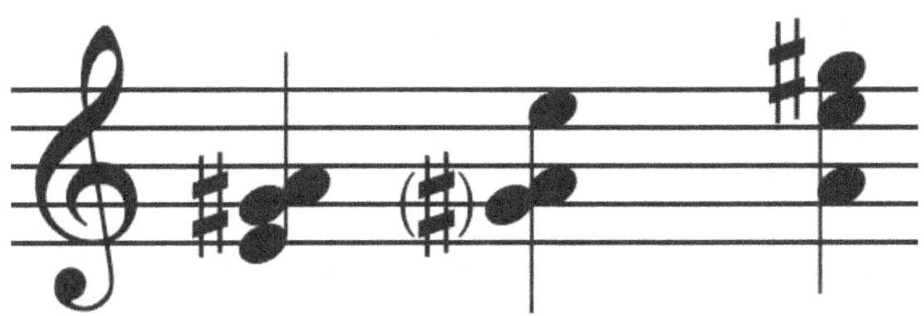

015 Retrograde "045"

015 Vector

In this vector trichord, I chose to stack intervals 1-5 over the bass note, but again you can do any combination of intervals from the vector.

0156 Symm Tetrachord

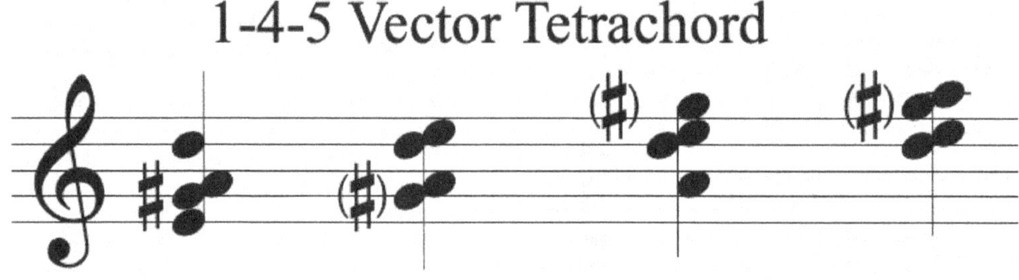

We can make the 015 symmetrical by adding a 1 to the end of it.

1-4-5 Vector Tetrachord

In this example I stacked the vector as 4-1-5 from note to note to create this tetrachord.

51015 Symm Pentachord

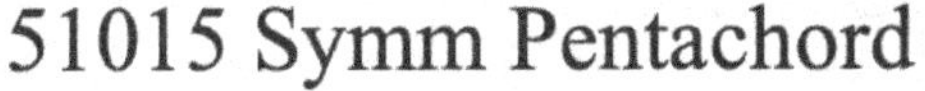

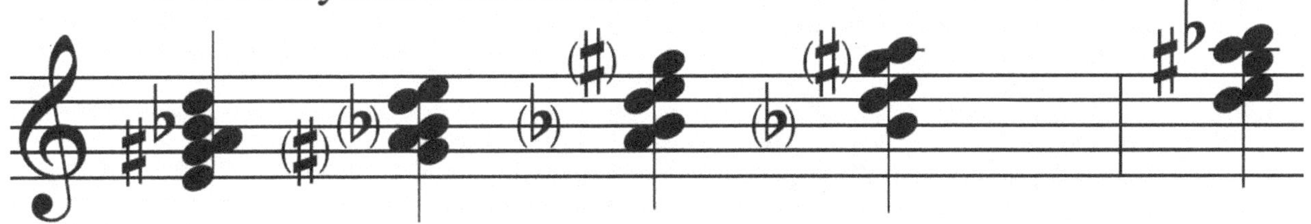

A is the center pitch 0, moving 1-5 in both directions creating this symmetrical pentachord.

You can also use the retrograde 045 for any of these tetrachords or pentachords.

Pairs of Pairs

As I mentioned before, the trichord 015 contains 3 interval pairs of 1-4 1-5 4-5.

1-4 / 1-5 Pair of Pair - Alternation

1-4 / 1-5 Pair of Pair - Pattern (1-1-4-1-1-5)

Cell and Linking Interval

In this example we go up 1-5 then down 4 as our cell, and down 1 for the linking interval.

Reconstruction

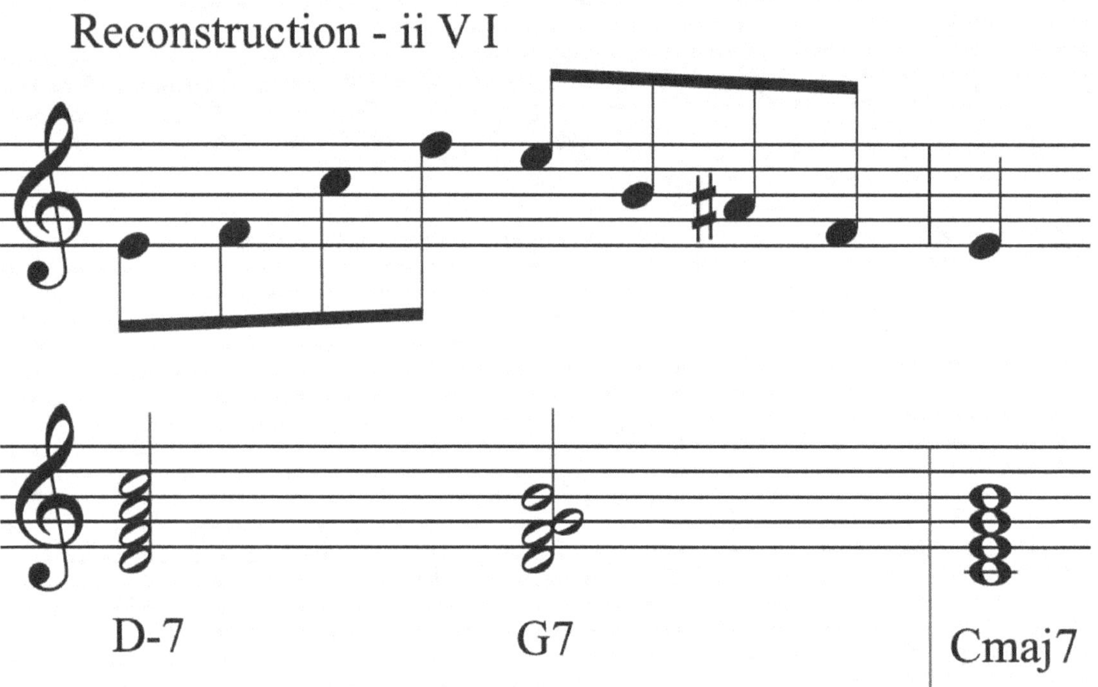

This reconstructed ii V I line only uses intervals from the 015 vector of 1-4-5. I utilized octave equivalence from F to C giving us the interval of 7.

016

Our fourth trichord has these three intervals contained in it.

1 = Minor Second

5 = Perfect Fifth

6 = Tritone

Which means its interval vector is 1-5-6.

So, we can have singulars of 1-1-1 giving us the fully chromatic scale, or 5-5-5 giving us quartal arpeggios, or 6-6-6 giving us tritone arpeggios, or any kind of alternation of the three like 1-4-1-4 or 1-5-1-5 or 4-5-4-5.

Which also means that there are 3 interval pairs of 1-5 1-6 5-6.

Literal

-Practice Shape 1

016 up, then 016 down.

Vector

1-5-6 up, then 1-5-6 down.

Chords

016 Literal

016 Retrograde "056"

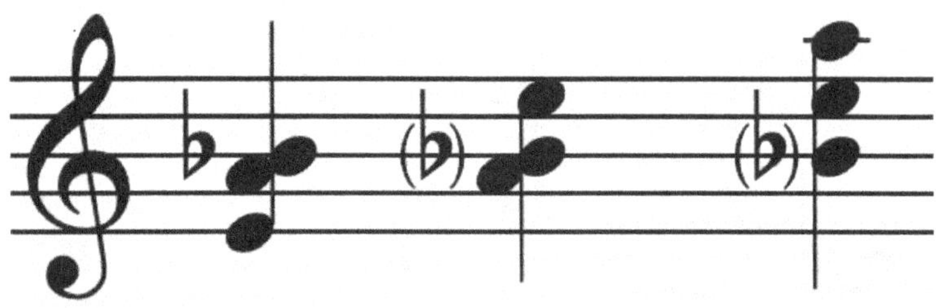

016 Vector

In this vector trichord, I chose to stack intervals 1-6 over the bass note, but again you can do any combination of intervals from the vector.

0167 Symm Tetrachord

We can make the 016 symmetrical by adding a 1 to the end of it.

1-5-6 Vector Tetrachord

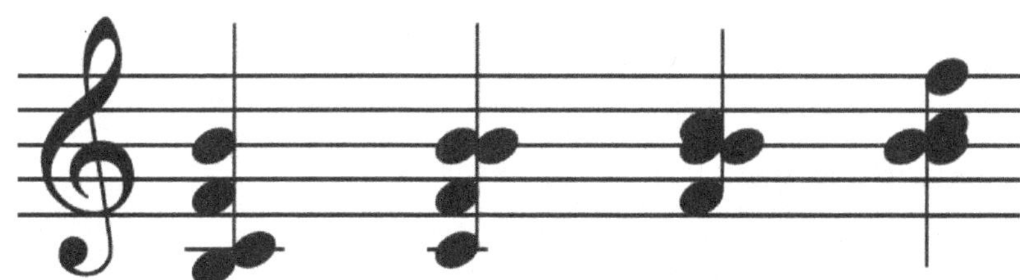

In this example I stacked the vector as 1-5-6 from note to note to create this tetrachord. The unison Bs are a bit unfortunate, however you could raise one B up another octave to avoid this.

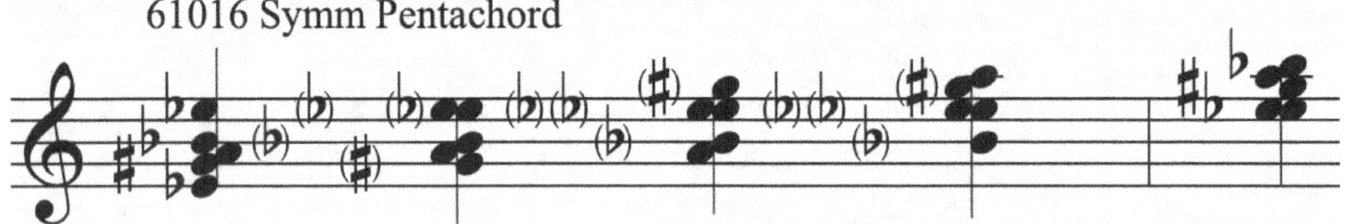

A is the center pitch 0, moving 1-6 in both directions creating this symmetrical pentachord. Again, we have an unfortunate repeated note. Interval 6 typically presents us with this issue.

You can also use the retrograde 056 for any of these tetrachords or pentachords.

Pairs of Pairs

As I mentioned before, the trichord 016 contains 3 interval pairs of   1-5   1-6   5-6.

1-5 / 1-6 Pair of Pair - Alternation

1-5 / 1-6 Pair of Pair - Pattern (1-1-5-1-1-6)

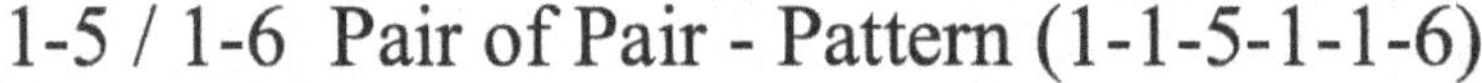

<h1 style="text-align:center">Cell and Linking Interval</h1>

Cell (6-1-5) + Linking Interval (1)

In this example we go up 6-1 then down 5 as our cell, and up 1 for the linking interval.

<h1 style="text-align:center">Reconstruction</h1>

Reconstruction - ii V I

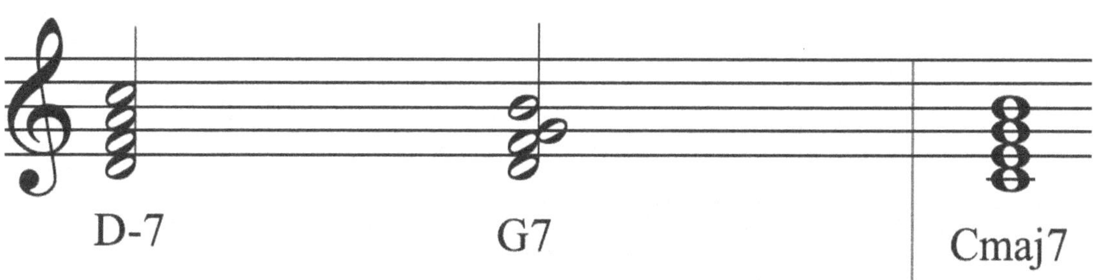

This reconstructed ii V I line only uses intervals from the 016 vector of 1-5-6.

025

Our fifth trichord has these three intervals contained in it.

2 = Major Second

3 = Minor Third

5 = Perfect Fourth

Which means its interval vector is 2-3-5.

So, we can have singulars of 2-2-2 giving us the whole-tone scale, or 3-3-3 giving us diminished arpeggios, or 5-5-5 giving us quartal arpeggios, or any kind of alternation of the three like 2-3-2-3 or 2-5-2-5 or 3-5-3-5.

Which also means that there are 3 interval pairs of 2-3 2-5 3-5.

Literal

-Practice Shape 1

025 up, then 025 down.

Vector

-Practice Shape 2

Chords

025 Literal

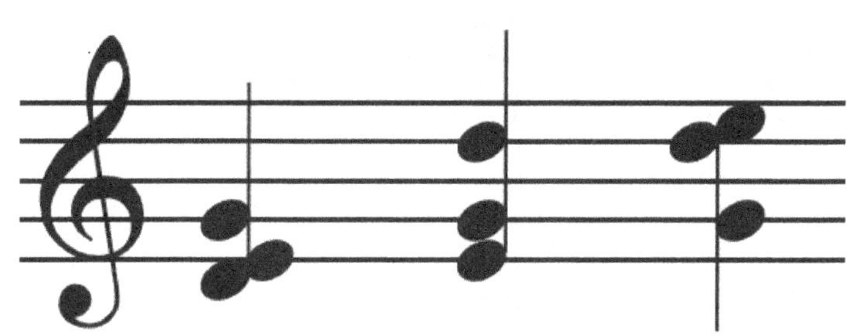

025 Retrograde "035"

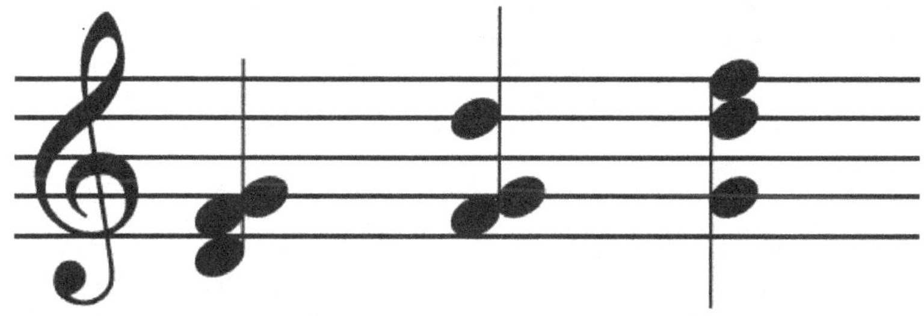

025 Vector

In this vector trichord, I chose to stack intervals 2-5 over the bass note, but again you can do any combination of intervals from the vector.

0257 Symm Tetrachord

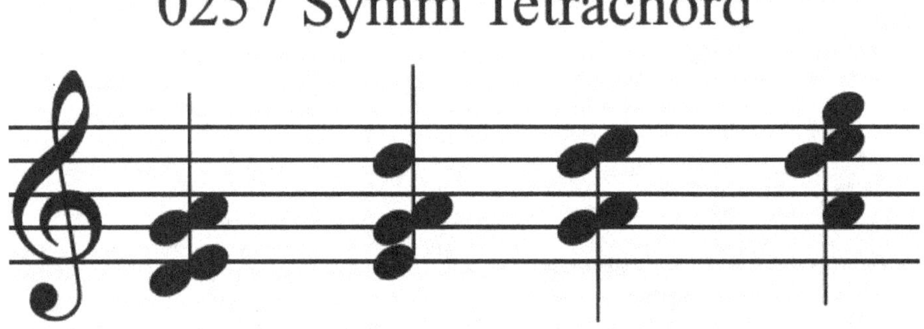

We can make the 025 symmetrical by adding a 2 to the end of it.

2-3-5 Vector Tetrachord

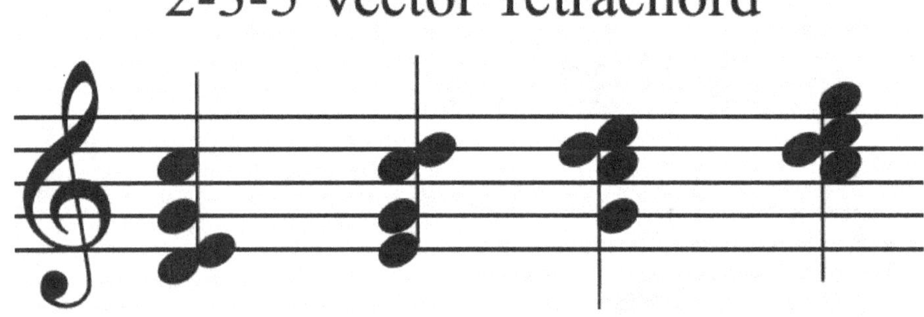

2-3-5 consecutively stacked from note to note.

52025 Symm Pentachord

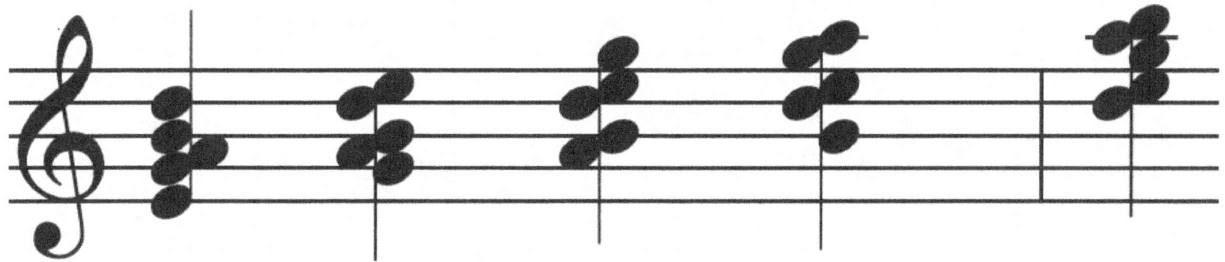

A is the center pitch 0, moving 2-5 in both directions creating this symmetrical pentachord.

You can also use the retrograde 035 for any of these tetrachords or pentachords.

Pairs of Pairs

As I mentioned before, the trichord 025 contains 3 interval pairs of   2-3   2-5   3-5.

2-3 / 2-5 Pair of Pair - Alternation

2-3 / 2-5 Pair of Pair - Pattern (2-2-3-2-2-5)

Cell and Linking Interval

In this example we go up 2-3-5 as our cell, and down 5 for the linking interval.

Reconstruction

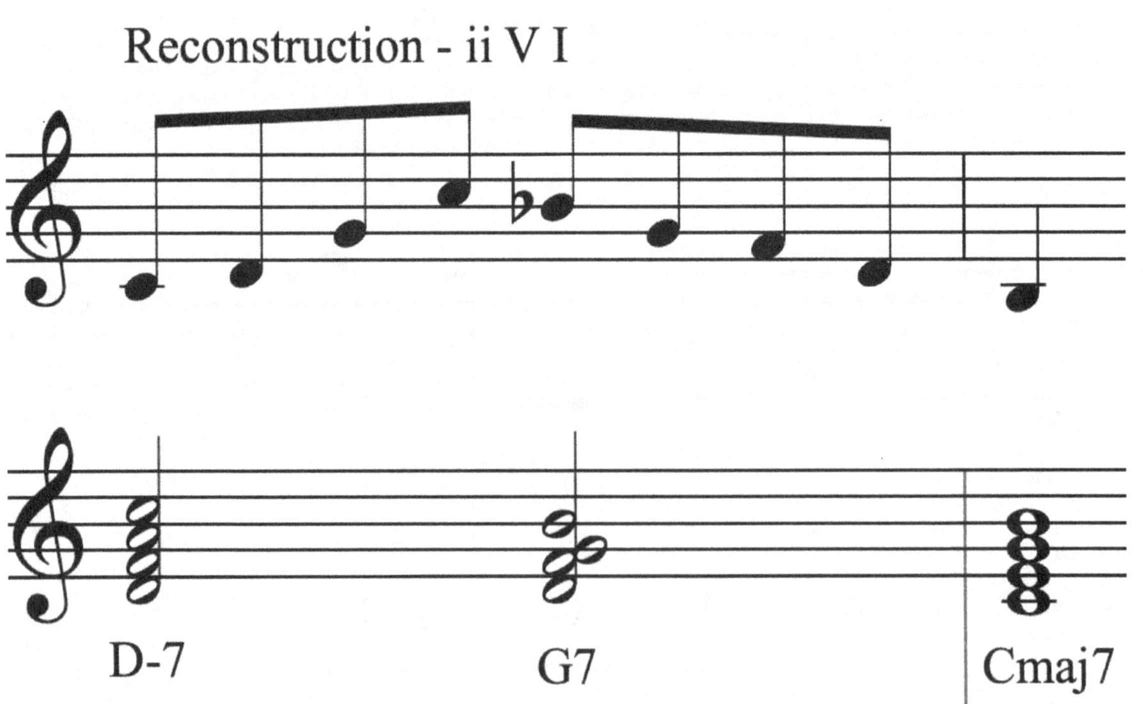

This reconstructed ii V I line only uses intervals from the 025 vector of 2-3-5.

026

Our sixth trichord has these three intervals contained in it.

2 = Major Second

4 = Major Third

6 = Tritone

Which means its interval vector is 2-4-6.

So, we can have singulars of 2-2-2 giving us the whole-tone scale, or 4-4-4 giving us augmented arpeggios, or 6-6-6 giving us tritone arpeggios, or any kind of alternation of the three like 2-4-2-4 or 2-6-2-6 or 4-6-4-6.

Which also means that there are 3 interval pairs of 2-4 2-6 4-6.

This one is the most difficult and limiting to work with out of all the trichords. In order to avoid being trapped in a small set of pitches, you may divide the intervals of 2 and 6 in half to utilize an occasional 1 or 3 to move to new unused pitches.

Literal

-Practice Shape 1

026 up, then 026 down.

<h1 style="text-align:center">Vector</h1>

-Practice Shape 2

2-4-6 up, then 2-4-6 down.

<h1 style="text-align:center">Chords</h1>

026 Literal

026 Retrograde "046"

026 Vector

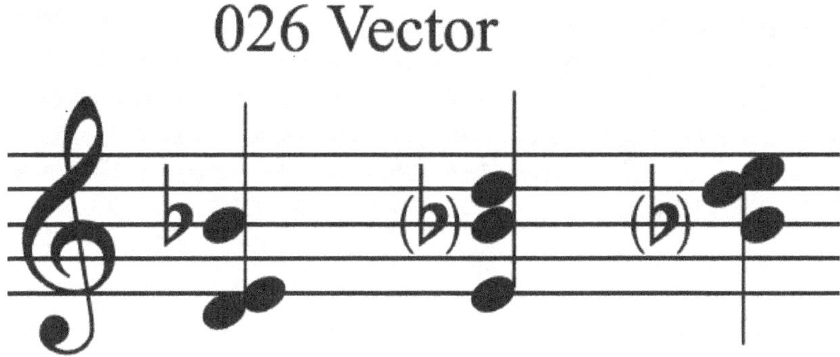

In this vector trichord, I chose to stack intervals 2-6 over the bass note, but again you can do any combination of intervals from the vector.

0268 Symm Tetrachord

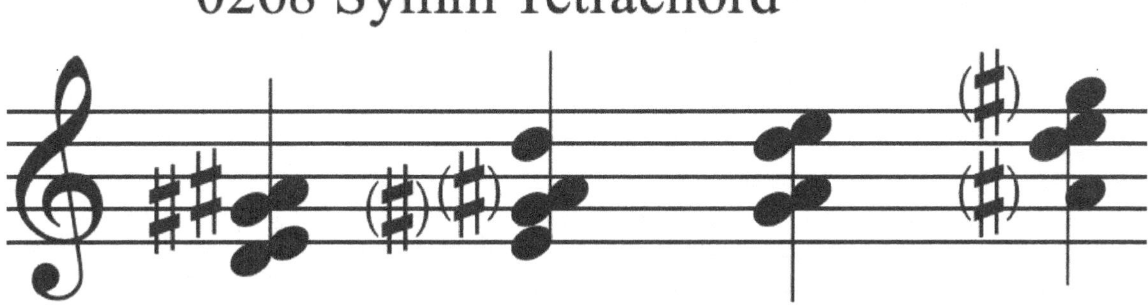

We can make the 026 symmetrical by adding a 2 to the end of it.

2-4-6 Vector Tetrachord

2-4-6 consecutively stacked from note to note. Another unfortunate unison.

62026 Symm Pentachord

A is the center pitch 0, moving 2-6 in both directions creating this symmetrical pentachord.

You can also use the retrograde 046 for any of these tetrachords or pentachords.

Pairs of Pairs

As I mentioned before, the trichord 026 contains 3 interval pairs of 2-4 2-6 4-6.

2-4 / 2-6 Pair of Pair - Alternation

2-4 / 2-6 Pair of Pair - Pattern (2-2-4-2-2-6)

<h1 style="text-align:center">Cell and Linking Interval</h1>

Cell (4-6-2) + Linking Interval (4)

In this example we go up 4-6 up then down 2 as our cell, and down 4 for the linking interval. This one repeats up an octave after 3 cycles.

<h1 style="text-align:center">Reconstruction</h1>

Reconstruction - ii V I

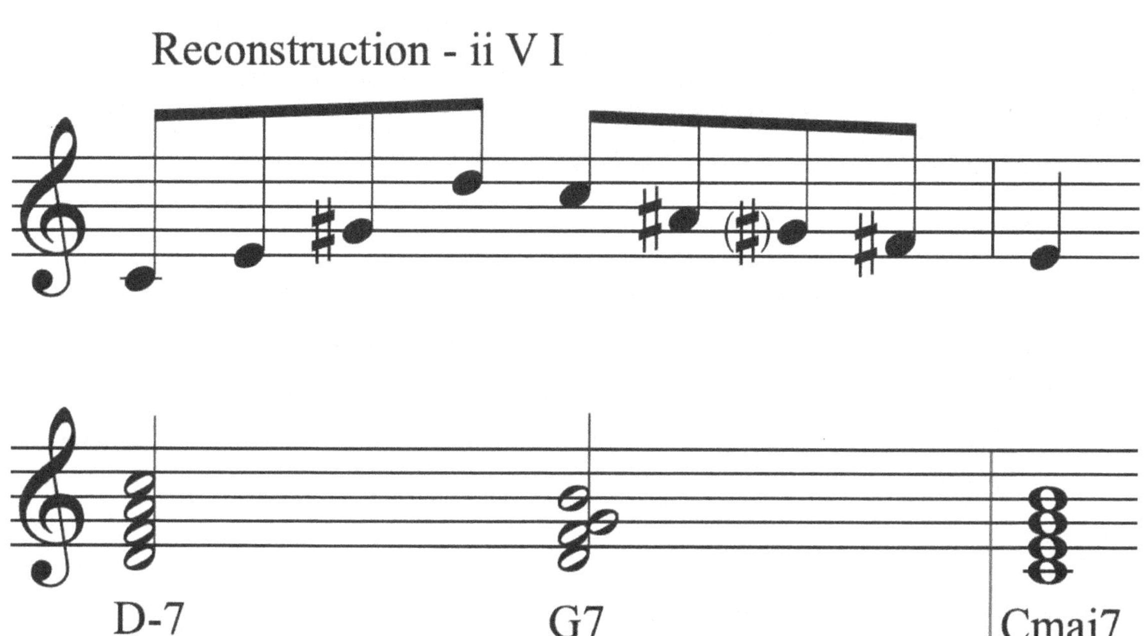

This reconstructed ii V I line only uses intervals from the 026 vector of 2-4-6.

Trichord Substitutions

Most jazz musicians are familiar with the concept of chord substitutions. A chord substitution is essentially inserting a different chord over a chord in the changes.

For example: Bø or "B-7b5" and Bb7 are typical chord substitutions for G7.

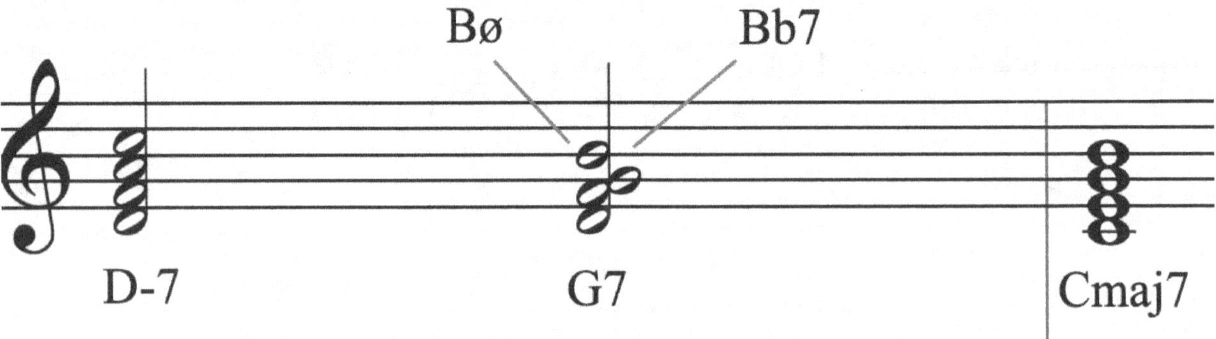

Every type of chord has its own list of typical chord substitutions. One of the most common ones is the tritone substitution. In place of G7, you use Db7 as a substitution. Db is a tritone away from G. In the spirit of jazz and the tritone substitution, I'd like to introduce you to the *Trichord Substitution*.

The name pretty much gives it away, but a Trichord Substitution is when we use a trichord in place of a normal chord. There isn't really a perfect way to choose which trichords work over each chord type. However, my advice is to find the interval vector of your "normal" chords and pick a trichord that shares some of those same intervals.

For example: G7 = G-B-D-F, and its interval vector is 2-3-4-5-6. So, you could use 026, 025, 023, 045 etc...

Of course, I always try to reduce the larger and retrograde trichords to the smaller original form, so 023 is 013 and 045 is 015.

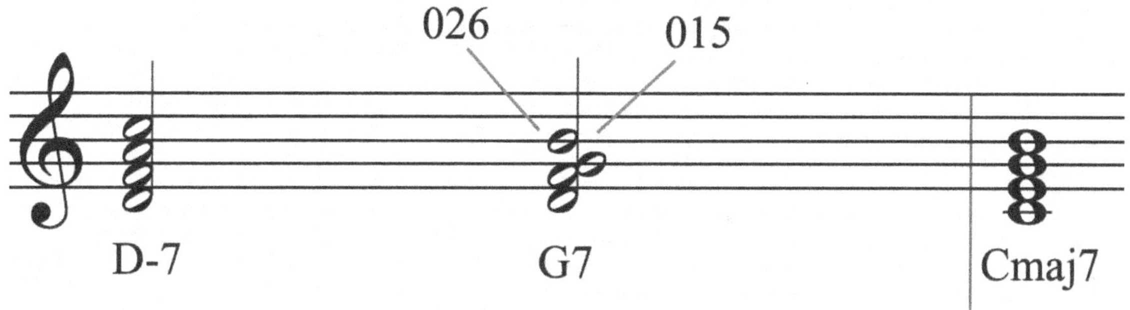

This is a really good place to start incorporating trichords into jazz changes. The V7 chord is typically the chord to play "outside" the harmony or use tritone subs.

That being said, if I have these 2 trichords in my chart over G7, I would use the trichord symbols G26 or G15. This shows me the root note and trichord type.

I have found this to be extremely effective and fairly easy to navigate even when my entire chart is trichords with root notes in place of 0. Here is an example of some typical changes you may know, all as trichord + root note chord symbols.

Trichord Substitution Etude

Trichord Substitution List

Here is a list of how I typically choose which trichords to use over chord types.

Maj7 = 014, 015

Min7 = 025

Dom7 = 015, 016, 026

Dim7 / half-Dim7 = 013, 014, 016

I tend to use trichords with 6 for dominant chords, since the tritone is typically what gives the dominant chords its tension. I also like to think about which tensions, (9, 11, 13 or b9, b5, b13) are in the dominant chords. Typically, in jazz we have different dominant chords for Maj7 and Min7 resolutions. Major chord resolutions will usually have the natural tensions and minor chord resolutions will have the flat tensions. So, 026 would work better for major and 016 is better for minor. Natural 9 vs. b9 basically.

At the end of the day, you will always have more than one option, but this is how I think about it.

Reharmonization

Another jazz concept similar to chord substitutions is something called "Reharmonization". Which is more or less the same concept of substituting one chord for another. However, the main focus in reharmonization is to change the harmony under a melody note without altering the melody. For example, we can create some typical harmony under a commonly known melody like so.

Here we have a typical I vi ii V progression that has harmonized our melody. Now, imagine this is a lead sheet. It's showing us the "correct" chords to harmonize the melody with, but maybe we don't like it. We can change the chords to anything we want, as long as it still harmonizes well with the melody.

Here is an example of how we can "Reharmonize" the melody with a different progression of chords. The melody is exactly the same, but the harmony under it is different. We can use this same reharmonization technique with trichords.

The thought behind reharmonization is different because we have to maintain the integrity of the melody, but we get to improvise and compose new harmonies and chord structures to fit with it. This mainly applies to chordal instruments like piano or guitar, but you can use this technique to write for choir, horns or string sections as well. It is different than chord substitutions, because substitutions are typically something you use over written changes while playing lines or comping.

However, reharmonization is typically used in the arranging process, or for improvising chord melodies. So, we can arrange our own chord melodies and learn to reharmonize them with Trichordal harmony.

The simplest explanation of harmonizing a melody is that you take a melody note and turn it into a chord tone. If our melody note is E, then we can use E as the third of a C chord, or the minor third of C#min, or as the fifth of A or Amin.

We can do the same thing with our trichords. We can take the melody note and use it as one of the intervals in a trichord. If we use 014 as an example, we can use the note E as a 0 in E14, a 1 in D#14 or F14, or as a 4 in C14 or G#14.

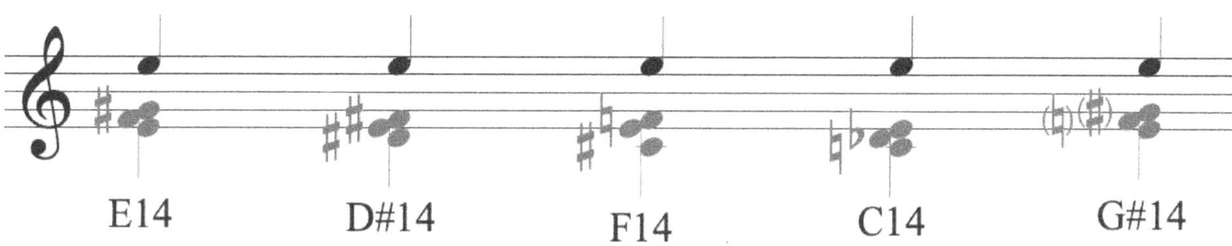

Dimensions of Related Trichords

Now we are going to makes things a bit more complicated. In the same vein of key centers and how keys are related to each other, trichords have relatives close and distant as well. The key of C's closest related keys are F and G, because they are only one accidental away from the key of C, but the keys of F# and C# are very distant sharing practically no common tones.

In the Atonal world of trichords, I call this *Degrees of Separation*. 0 degrees of separation is what I call *Factor 0*. Factor 0 is the original trichord, and each additional interval beyond the original trichord is an additional factor. 1 interval beyond the original trichord is *Factor 1* (1 degree of separation), and 2 intervals away is *Factor 2* (2 degrees of separation).

I know it sounds confusing, but look at the first visual chart. Basically, C13 is the original trichord as Factor 0, and trichords built around the 1 interval distance away from C are Factor 1. So, B13, A13, Db13, and Eb13 are the Factor 1 related trichords to C13.

(Notes move 1-3 in both directions from 0.)

Factor 2 is moving 1-3 from the center of the F1 trichords. So, our F2 trichords are D13, E13, Gb13, Ab13, and Bb13. Each of those roots are either a 1 or 3 away from the F1 roots, and F1 roots are either a 1 or 3 away from the F0 root.

Some trichords are repeated in upper factors, but my lists do not carry them over. For example, the note C can be found in F2, which means theoretically C13 should be a trichord in F2. However, since C13 is our original F0 trichord, we would not carry it over in the list of F2 trichords.

Dimensions of Related Trichords

013

Factor 2
Outer Square

3/C	3/D		3/E	3/Gb
1/Bb	1/C		1/D	1/E
3/A	1/B	0/C	1/Db	3/Eb
1/Ab	1/Bb		1/C	1/D
3/Gb	3/Ab		3/Bb	3/C

Factor 1

Inner Square

Factor = x degrees of separation

Factor 0 = original trichord C13

Factor 1 = 1 degree of separation, 1 interval from centor

Factor 2 = 2 degree of separation, 2 intervals from center

(Fixed)

Factor 1 Trichords = Db13, Eb13, A13, B13

Factor 2 Trichords = D13, E13, Gb13, Ab13, Bb13

(Transposable)

Factor 1 Trichords = 113, 313, 914, L13

Factor 2 Trichords = 213, 413, 613, 813, T13

(T = 10, L = 11)

Factor 1 is closely related to Factor 0, and Factor 2 is more distantly related to Factor 0. Although Factor 2 is distant to Factor 0, it is closely related to Factor 1.

So, if a chart shows C13, use factor 0 to play "in" the chord, factor 1 to be a little "out", and factor 2 to sound even "more out". I call this *Factorial Superimposition*.

See C13, play Db13, Eb13, B13, A13 for Factor 1.

See C13, play D13, E13, Gb13, Ab13, Bb13 for Factor 2.

Dimensions of Related Trichords
014

Factor 2

Outer Square

4/C	4/Eb		4/F	4/Ab
1/A	1/C		1/D	1/F
4/Ab	1/B	0/C	1/Db	4/E
1/G	1/Bb		1/C	1/Eb
4/E	4/G		4/A	4/C

Factor 1

Inner Square

Factor = x degrees of separation
Factor 0 = original trichord C14
Factor 1 = 1 degree of separation, 1 interval from center
Factor 2 = 2 degrees of separation, 2 intervals from center

(Fixed)
Factor 1 Trichords = Db14, E14, Ab14, B14
Factor 2 Trichords = D14, Eb14, F14, G14, A14, Bb14

(Transposable)
Factor 1 Trichords = 114, 414, 814, L14
Factor 2 Trichords = 214, 314, 514, 714, 914, T14

(T = 10, L = 11)

Dimensions of Related Trichords
015

Factor 2
Outer Square

5/C	5/E		5/Gb	5/Bb
1/Ab	1/C		1/D	1/Gb
5/G	1/B	0/C	1/Db	5/F
1/Gb	1/Bb		1/C	1/E
5/D	5/Gb		5/Ab	5/C

Factor 1

Inner Square

Factor = x degrees of separation
Factor 0 = original trichord C15
Factor 1 = 1 degree of separation, 1 interval from center
Factor 2 = 2 degrees of separation, 2 intervals from center

(Fixed)
Factor 1 Trichords = Db15, F15, G15, B15
Factor 2 Trichords = D15, E15, Gb15, Ab15, Bb15

(Transposable)
Factor 1 Trichords = 115, 515, 715, L15
Factor 2 Trichords = 215, 415, 615, 815, T15

(T = 10, L = 11)

Dimensions of Related Trichords
016

Factor 2
Outer Square

6/C	6/F		6/G	6/C	
1/G	1/C		1/D	1/G	
6/Gb	1/B	0/C	1/Db	6/Gb	
1/F	1/Bb		1/C	1/F	
6/C	6/F		6/G	6/C	

Factor 1
Inner Square

Factor = x degrees of separation

Factor 0 = original trichord 016

Factor 1 = 1 degree of separation, 1 interval from center

Factor 2 = 2 degrees of separation, 2 intervals from center

(Fixed)
Factor 1 Trichords = Db16, Gb16, B16
Factor 2 Trichords = D16, F15, G16, Bb16

(Transposable)
Factor 0 Trichords = 116, 616, L16
Factor 1 Trichords = 216, 516, 716, T16

(T = 10, L = 11)

Dimensions of Related Trichords
025

Factor 2
Outer Square

5/C	5/Eb		5/G	5/Bb	
2/A	2/C		2/E	2/G	
5/G	2/Bb	0/C	2/D	5/F	
2/F	2/Ab		2/C	2/Eb	
5/D	5/F		5/A	5/C	

Factor 1
Inner Square

Factor = x degrees of separation
Factor 0 = original trichord C25
Factor 1 = 1 degree of separation, 1 interval from center
Factor 2 = 2 degrees of separation, 2 intervals from center

(Fixed)
Factor 1 Trichords = D25, F25, G25, Bb25
Factor 2 Trichords = Eb25, E25, Ab25, A25

(Transposable)
Factor 1 Trichords = 225, 525, 725, T25
Factor 2 Trichords = 325, 425, 825, 925

(T = 10, L = 11)

Dimensions of Related Trichords
026

Factor 2
Outer Square

6/C	6/E		6/Ab	6/C
2/Ab	2/C		2/E	2/Ab
6/Gb	2/Bb	0/C	2/D	6/Gb
2/E	2/Ab		2/C	2/E
6/C	6/E		6/Ab	6/C

Factor 1

Inner Square

Factor = x degrees of separation

Factor 0 = original trichord C26

Factor 1 = 1 degree of separation, 1 interval from center

Factor 2 = 2 degrees of separation, 2 intervals from center

(Fixed)

Factor 1 Trichords = D26, Gb26, Bb26

Factor 2 Trichords = E26, Ab26

(Transposable)

Factor 1 Trichords = 226, 626, T26

Factor 2 Trichords = 426, 826

(T = 10, L = 11)

Review of Terms

Trichord Substitution – Substituting trichords for normal chords.

Reharmonization – Using trichords to reharmonize a melody or progression.

Degrees of Separation – Number of intervals from center of original trichord.

Factor – Degrees of separation away from center of original trichord.

Factorial Superimposition – Superimposing factorial related trichords.

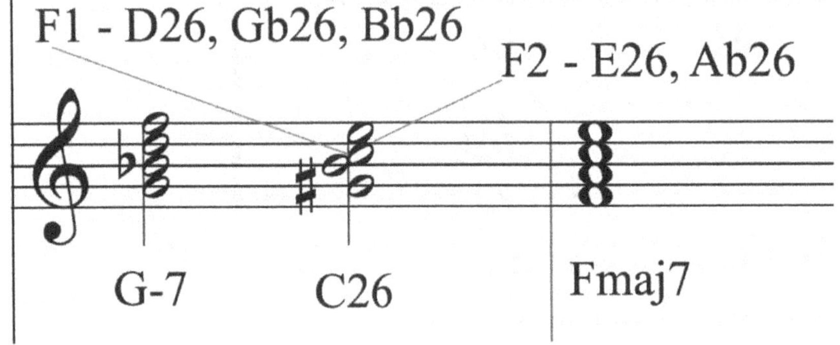

Dimensions of Related Trichords

ETC

4	4	4	4	
1	1	1	1	Factor 2
	4		4	Factor 1
	1		1	
0	1	4		Factor 0

Rhythmic and Metric Possibilities

We have not mentioned anything about meter or rhythm so far. The word "Atonal" only refers to "tone" as in pitch or "tonal" center. However, if we want to talk about meter and rhythm, we could use terms like" Ametric" or "Arhythmic". There are many possibilities for Ametric and Arhythmic uses of interval pairs and trichords.

You can assign a value to 1 (like 16th notes) and apply that to all the trichords and interval pairs. For example:

This would be an example of *Durational Rhythms*. You can assign any duration you desire to 1 and apply it as such. 16th = 1, 32nd = 1, or 8th triplet = 1. Etc...

You could also apply the intervallic numbers to note groupings. 1-3 would be groupings of 1 and 3 notes. For example:

And metrically, you could use *Compound-Meters*.

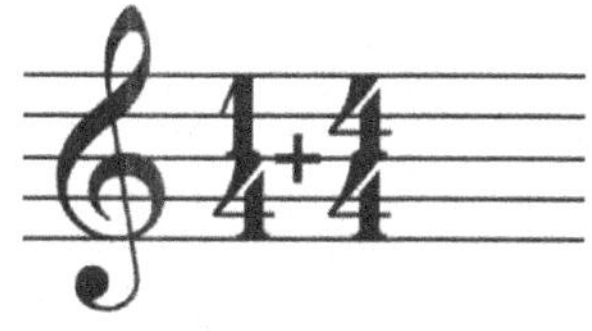

For example: 1-4 = 1 / 4 + 4 / 4

Improvisation Exercises

Much of my improvisational experimentation with interval pairs and trichords has been in a duo setting and with a loop or delay pedal. So, I came up with a few exercises to help myself and my duo partner to master the material and improvise together with more ease.

Constant Half Notes – Maintain constant half notes with pair or trichord. This works best with a delay pedal. I prefer feedback set to 0, but this is up to you.

Constant Quarter Notes – Maintain constant quarter notes with pair or trichord. (try different durations with delay pedal for constant note exercises)

Four notes then Hold – In 4 / 4, play four quarter notes, then one whole note. (players alternate who is playing quarter notes and whole notes)

One Bar Canon – With 2 players, 1st player plays a one measure canon and second player joins with their own canon second measure. Each canonic measure is played twice. With delay pedal, set duration to = 1 measure. So, each measure is played twice. Feedback should be set to 0 and level should be 100.

Alternating Counterpoint - With 2 players, in 4 / 4 one player plays beats 1-3 and the other player plays beats 2-4. With a delay pedal set to = 1 measure, play beats 1-3, then beats 2-4 in the next measure.

1 Bar line + 1 Bar Chords – With 2 players, player 1 starts with a 1 measure line, player 2 starts with 1 measure of chords, then alternate. Same idea with delay pedal set to 1 measure duration. Alternate 1 bar line, then 1 bar chords.

Composition

Even though this book has primarily focused on jazz, all of these techniques can be used in their own right. Interval Pairs and Trichords can be used to compose and improvise with in any context. All the pieces for our guitar duo were written with trichords. I have also composed full pieces with trichords, including a string quartet and Messiaen quartet called "Impromptu". Here are some examples of compositions that use trichords and improvisation in a non-jazz context.

In Composition #1 we alternate which player is improvising and which player is playing the accompaniment. Player 1 plays the A theme while Player 2 improvises with 025 over it. Composition #2 has a more complicated form, but only uses 015.

Closing Thoughts

This material is very difficult to master. It will take years of exploration and practice to become a fluent improviser of interval pairs and trichords. Even for myself, I have been working on this material for about 3 years now and I still feel like a beginner with it.

Let's sum up a visual list of our essential interval pairs and trichords. There are 9 interval pairs and 6 trichords. Making our list a total of 15 intervallic structures.

Interval Pairs

1-3 1-4 1-5 1-6

2-3 2-5 2-6

3-4 3-5

Trichords

013 014 015 016

025 026

Just remember, the most efficient way to get better is to write your own etudes and compose your own ideas. I hope you enjoyed this book and have fun playing!

About The Author

Jared E. Davis is a composer, guitarist and teacher. His interests range from a deep respect for J.S. Bach, a passion for early atonality and a nostalgic love of classic rock. His current goal is to expand the palette of contemporary-classical music by integrating it with a multitude of other styles, such as rock, jazz, funk, and fusion. He also draws a wider audience to art music itself, through live new music performances at intimate venues.

As a self-taught guitarist, he began performing at age 16 by forming his own band. After finishing his 4 years of service in the US Navy, he was accepted into Berklee College of Music in Boston, where he received his BM in Guitar Performance in 2019. While studying performance, he quickly realized his real passion was for composition and in 2021 received his MM in Music Composition from Texas State University.

Currently, Jared has authored two other books, "Chromatic Ladders" and "Music Theory For Fretboarders", premiered new works with SMART Orchestra, Unheard-of Ensemble, and gives lectures and performances with The Atonal Guitar Duo.

www.ingramcontent.com/pod-product-compliance
Lightning Source LLC
Chambersburg PA
CBHW081929120726
47997CB00010B/3096